HITLER'S HENCHMEN

Patrick Morgan

HITLER'S HENCHMEN

First published in the UK in 2012

© Demand Media Limited 2012

www.demand-media.co.uk

Printed and bound in China

ISBN 978-1-909217-18-8

Contents

4 – 7   Introduction

8 – 17   Joseph Goebbels

18 – 27   Hermann Goering

28 – 37   Rudolf Hess

38 – 47   Heinrich Himmler

48 – 57   Karl Doenitz

58 – 67   Albert Speer

68 – 77   Adolf Eichmann

78 – 87   Martin Bormann

88 – 97   Baldur von Schirach

98 – 107   Joachim von Ribbentrop

108 – 117 Dr Josef Mengele

118 – 127 Roland Freisler

Inroduction

Adolf Hitler, the man who led Germany to ruin in World War II and who, humiliated and depressed, killed himself in a bunker beneath the battle-torn streets of Berlin, had once had rather grander ideas for his adopted country.

The Austrian-born Führer had envisaged a Germany that enjoyed imperial dominance over continental Europe and the ability to subject its peoples to the totalitarian, single-party ideology of Nazism. One day, Hitler had imagined, his New Order would grow to rule the entire world.

He had had other dreams, among them the breeding of a master race of 'Aryan' supermen and superwomen, which would involve the elimination of 'impure' blood in the German people. Hitler also thought it essential that his imagined enemies of the master race – communists and the Jewish people –

should be eliminated.

The Germans had to have lebensraum (living space), he had theorised, and that was why he had dreamed of expanding the nation's boundaries ever wider, crushing or moving on the populations that stood in the way.

Hitler set out his dreams and ambitions in Mein Kampf (My Struggle), which he dictated while he was serving a prison term for his leading part in the attempted coup d'état of 1923 that came to be known as the Beer Hall Putsch. But he had begun to formulate

INTRODUCTION

his political ideas much earlier, as he grew up, fought in World War I and saw post-war Germany humiliated by the Treaty of Versailles.

His ideas were taking more coherent shape as he joined the German Workers' Party in 1919 and went on to become leader of its successor, the National Socialist German Workers' Party, or NSDAP (better known as the Nazis) in 1921. But Hitler realised he would need around him an iron-strong coterie of extraordinarily dedicated, devoted, talented and ruthless men – plus the occasional woman – if his dreams were to be realised.

One of the men he chose was Rudolf Hess, the man who rose to become the Führer's deputy and to whom Hitler dictated Mein Kampf. In 1941 Hess ruined his reputation by flying on a solo peace mission to Scotland. He never saw Hitler again and died a lonely man in prison.

Another of Hitler's intimate circle was Joseph Goebbels, a gifted orator and propagandist who never missed a chance to promote the Nazi world view, or his own interests. A man who fitted the henchman description perfectly was Hermann Goering, a swaggering flying ace who headed Hitler's air force, the Luftwaffe, and became his second-in-command.

Heinrich Himmler, a man of infinite cruelty and head of the SS and Waffen-SS organisations, was Germany's most feared man. He was also one of the prime influences behind the Nazis' Final Solution to the Jewish question, which turned into genocide. Adolf Eichmann was the bureaucrat who organised the Holocaust, shuffling humans around Europe and into gas chambers as if they were pawns on a chessboard.

Grand Admiral Karl Doenitz, when he was put on trial after the war, denied all knowledge of the extermination of the Jews and other peoples. He did, though, admit responsibility for his U-boats' murderous tactics against Allied and merchant shipping.

Germany's war economy was the domain of Albert Speer, a brilliant architect whose genius for organisation took him to the top. Also intent on a position close to Hitler was Martin Bormann, whose readiness to stab his comrades in the back paid dividends.

Baldur von Schirach was the cultured theatre director's son who, as the head of the Hitler Youth, taught millions of young Germans to love the Führer and despise Jews. Joachim von Ribbentrop was a ridiculous incompetent, a foreign minister who knew nothing about foreign affairs and displayed his ignorance for the world to see.

Josef Mengele's macabre experiments on living people at the Auschwitz extermination camp, perpetrated in the name of science, earned him the title of the Doctor of Death. Roland Freisler was the demented, bawling judge of the People's Court who condemned thousands to death on the gallows or at the guillotine for the pettiest of crimes.

Hitler's henchmen formed a real-life chamber of horrors, each one responsible for perpetuating the lies of the Nazi regime and condemning millions to premature death.

Some fled from justice, others paid for their crimes. Some remained committed to the Führer's ideals, others saw the light. Some regretted the enormous death toll of the war and Holocaust, others delighted in the ending of lives. But each one was possessed of an intriguing personality.

Chapter 1

Goebbels -
The Firebrand

Was there ever such a dedicated propagandist as Joseph Goebbels, the man who convinced the German people of the justness of Hitler's Nazi crusade against the Jews and war against non-believers? The Minister of Propaganda's cruelly efficient manipulation of the press and radio, cynical use of slogans and films and suppression of opinion pointed to a man who was utterly single-minded in his determination to succeed at any cost.

Goebbels was among the most outspoken anti-Semites within the Nazi party, and the relish with which he directed drives to deprive them of rights, liberty and life was always evident. Disliked by colleague and foe alike, he was a little man who strove constantly to rise to the top.

And he did just that, becoming Plenipotentiary for Total War after the Nazis' eastern front crumbled and Russian forces neared Berlin. Such was his commitment to the cause, and to Hitler, that he stayed with the Führer to the end and was named Reich Chancellor after his death.

His use of propaganda was based on a simple belief that you could fool all of the people all of the time if you were thorough, bold and ruthless enough. 'If you tell a lie big enough and keep repeating it, people will eventually come to believe it,' he wrote in his diary. 'The lie can be maintained only

"*The truth is the enemy of the State.*"

for such time as the State can shield the people from the political, economic and/or military consequences of the lie.

'It then becomes vitally important for the State to use all of its powers to repress dissent, for the truth is the mortal enemy of the lie, and thus by extension, the truth is the greatest enemy of the State.'

Joseph Goebbels was born on 29 October 1897 in the Prussian town of Rheydt, to a father who was a factory clerk and a mother who had been a farm worker before marriage. One of five children raised in the Catholic faith, he was handicapped from an early age by a deformed right leg resulting from an attack of polio. He was to suffer a sense of physical inadequacy

– also stemming from his lack of height – for the rest of his life.

Goebbels studied history and literature at the University of Heidelberg and, wanting to enlist in the German army to fight in World War I, was crushed when he was turned down because of his disability. A brooding resentment over this rejection was compounded when the terms of the Treaty of Versailles led to the humiliation, as he saw it, of Germany. By the early 1920s he was a bitter man, and like many of his kind he joined the Nazi Party as it began its rise to power in 1922.

Goebbels bore little resemblance to the 'Aryan' stereotype – blond, strong, fit and healthy – portrayed by the Nazis as the natural masters of all races. Small, dark-haired, obviously disabled and of an intellectual bent, he set out to compensate for his shortcomings by imposing his will on those he regarded as inferior – and there is plenty of

RIGHT University of Heidelberg logo

evidence to suggest that Goebbels regarded almost everybody as inferior to himself. His resentment, inner rage and self-hatred were raised to new levels when his efforts to become known for his literary talents were ignored by indifferent publishers. Just one novel, Michael: ein Deutsches Schicksal in Tagebuchblattern, found its way to the bookshelves.

Naturally, given the Nazis' antipathy towards Jews, whom they regarded as the creators of all the misfortune to have befallen Germany, Goebbels' hatred focused on that race as he rose through the party. By the mid-1920s he was displaying extraordinary powers of oratory and communication as well as sharp political instinct and the ability to better himself whenever the opportunity arose.

His speaking skills were unlike those of Hitler; he rarely ranted, relying instead on passion, sarcasm, lies and insinuation to win over his audience, and his deep voice belied his diminutive stature.

In 1925 he became business manager of the Nazis' Ruhr district, and it was shortly afterwards that the Führer gained an early insight into Goebbels' ruthlessness: at a conference in 1926 he called for the expulsion from the party of the 'petit bourgeois' Hitler. When Goebbels, who had previously occupied a position firmly within the left wing of the party, saw which way the wind was blowing, he shifted his allegiance to Hitler and stayed with him for ever after.

Appointed district leader for Berlin-Brandenburg, Goebbels went into overdrive in his surge to higher power, sweeping aside allies and enemies alike. He edited his own newspaper Der Angriff (The Attack), mounted impressive parades and poster and handbill campaigns and agitated by all means necessary; his corps of bodyguards were often involved in brawls and street battles as he advanced his personal agenda.

By this time his reputation for cynicism and opportunism was well known. He was despised in all quarters, known as the Poison Dwarf and 'a nightmare and goblin of history'. Still, even his opponents could not help but admire his talents and decisiveness.

Goebbels it was who most clearly articulated the National Socialist message – via slogans, speeches and slander – to a German population that was

BELOW Goebbels speaking in public

BELOW Goebbels at the side of Hitler

longing for an exit from the misery of desperate economic conditions and the humiliation of the terms of the Versailles Treaty. Goebbels knew exactly how to play on their hopes and

BELOW Goebbels at the side of Hitler

fears and how to hammer home the message. 'The essence of propaganda consists in winning people over to an idea so sincerely, so vitally, that in the end they succumb to it utterly and can never again escape from it,' he explained at a later date.

A further insight into his method came in the statement: 'The most brilliant propagandist technique will yield no success unless one fundamental principle is borne in mind constantly – it must confine itself to a few points and repeat them over and over.'

The idea Goebbels was communicating so effectively appealed to some of the German people's baser instincts: insecurity, xenophobia and class envy. He was so successful that Hitler had few alternatives when it came to appointing his party's propaganda leader. By 1929 Goebbels had arrived in the Nazis' inner circle.

Now he set about sowing the seeds of the Führer cult and watching as they grew and flourished. He portrayed Hitler as a quasi-superhuman, as the saviour of the German nation from the so-called international Jewish and Marxist conspiracies – despite having aligned himself with the Soviet cause earlier in his career. In the months preceding the Reichstag elections of 1932, which took Hitler to power, Goebbels' powers of persuasion were at their height as he attached himself ever closer, like a clinging limpet, to the future Führer's side.

His reward, given after Hitler was declared Chancellor in January 1933, was the post of Minister of Public Enlightenment and Propaganda. In fact, he had acted as if he had held that position since the 1932 elections. But his name was now on the office door and he was free to dispense poison from on high.

He was heading up a new ministry whose brief was to control every facet of communication and cultural life, including the arts and the mass media: the press, radio and cinema. 'Think of the press as a great keyboard on which the government can play,' he said, and he played with the authority of a master. And as he played, he marked out Germany's Jews for special attention.

He was undoubtedly mobilising huge anti-Semitic feeling (which was to culminate in the genocide that became known as the Holocaust) when he organised the mass burning of the works of Jewish authors in May 1933, but did he really harbour such personal hatred for Jews? Hermann Goering, in 1933 the founder of the Gestapo secret police and later commander-in-chief of the Luftwaffe, had his doubts.

'Goebbels was the strongest representative of anti-Semitism,' Goering

BELOW 1932 Reichstag elections

admitted to American psychiatrist Leon Goldensohn in 1946, before adding: 'He saw his big chance to become powerful by using the press for anti-

Semitic reasons.'

He continued: 'Personally, I think Goebbels was using anti-Semitism merely as a means of achieving personal power. Whether he had any deep-seated hatred against the Jews is questionable. I think he was too much of a thief and dishonest opportunist to have any deep-seated feelings for or against anything.

'But for years Goebbels had been trying in vain to become a big power. At last he saw his chance. He had whipped up anti-Semitic feelings to such a point by his vicious propaganda that he now thought he could do anything.

RIGHT Kristallnacht 1938

He probably didn't think about the consequences himself. He was a fanatic of an abnormal calibre.'

Goering added: 'You couldn't discuss anything with Goebbels … he was so dishonest that it didn't pay to discuss anything with him.'

Even if Goering was correct and Goebbels did not harbour any specific ill feeling towards the Jews, it is probably true to say that he did harbour a nameless animosity towards every one of his fellow humans. It is a pity he did not survive for a psychiatrist to bring to light the many complexes that drove him, but drive him they did, on an ever more destructive path.

He was the orchestrator and instigator of Kristallnacht, the one-night series of attacks on Jews and Jewish-owned buildings in 1938 that left 91 dead, 30,000 detained in concentration camps and a thousand synagogues in ruins. And he was one of the architects, in 1942, of the Final Solution, the Nazi plan to eradicate the Jews of Europe.

As the war broke out and continued, Hitler grew to trust and admire Goebbels more and more, turning to him when the German people needed yet more encouragement or persuasion that right was on their side. Even when Goebbels' ceaseless womanising had led to the threat of a marriage

BELOW Goebbels speaking in the Sports Palace, 1943

break-up in 1938 – unthinkable to the morally conservative Führer – Hitler had moved to solve the problem and smooth the way for his Propaganda Minister to continue his work.

And this he did during the war, using his control of all channels of information to rouse the people to ever greater fervour. In February 1943, in a Berlin speech that followed the Germans' catastrophic loss of the Battle of Stalingrad, Goebbels whipped up the audience into a frenzy as he insisted the nation should mobilise for total war. Surrender to the Allies was impossible, he proclaimed, and there were only two possible outcomes to the conflict: victory or annihilation.

By that time, with Hitler cutting down on his public appearances fol-lowing setbacks in the war, Goebbels was the public face of the government. It was a role he accepted with enthusiasm, for it represented a further advance on the road to ultimate power.

Hitler had further reason to thank Goebbels in July 1944, when the latter's decisive action helped to quell a plot to assassinate the Führer. His thanks came in the form of a position he had long worked towards: General Plenipotentiary for Total War. He now had complete authority to conduct the war on the home front, urging the people on to greater sacrifice in conditions that worsened by the day. It was too late to achieve much, apart from an increase in the number of German deaths. The Allies were on their way to Berlin.

In April 1945, Goebbels and his entire family moved into the Führerbunker beneath the Chancellery buildings, where Hitler was already installed. The move was symbolic of the closeness with Hitler that Goebbels had achieved after many years of manoeuvring.

Hitler and his mistress, Eva Braun, killed themselves on 30 April, as the Russians were closing in on the buildings. Under the terms of the

LEFT Goebbels family portrait: in the centre are Magda Goebbels and Joseph Goebbels, with their six children Helga, Hildegard, Helmut, Hedwig, Holdine and Heidrun. Behind is Harald Quandt in the uniform of a sergeant of the Air Force, 1 January 1944

late Führer's will, Goebbels was to be appointed the new Reich Chancellor, but the role had little meaning for Goebbels. He had already accepted death as the inevitable outcome of his final stand.

Some Nazi officials were plotting an escape from the bunker, but Goebbels refused to join them. On the evening of 1 May, he had his six children killed by a Nazi dentist, by morphine injection and cyanide.

Then Goebbels and his wife, Magda, went up to the gardens of the Chancellery. There, it is thought, he shot himself while Magda swallowed cyanide. The rule of the Poison Dwarf was over.

Chapter 2

Goering -
The Marshal

RIGHT Hermann Goering

Strutting, swaggering, self-obsessed, cruel beyond words and jostling for power and a position close to Hitler, Hermann Goering was the stereotype of the high-ranking Nazi. Add bizarre behaviour and incompetence to the mix and you have an image familiar from a hundred films and novels portraying Hitler's cronies as idiotic figures of fun.

But the real Goering was far from comic material. As the Führer's second-in-command and commander-in-chief of the German air force, he was responsible for the deaths of countless human beings, both in the Luftwaffe's bombing raids and in the gas chambers of the death camps.

Rising from an already privileged upbringing, he reached heroic status and an exalted position of power before his ignorance, drug addiction and megalomania brought the dream to an ignominious end. He finished his days alone, friendless, discredited and facing the hangman's noose.

He fancied he would be seen as a martyr for the Fatherland. It was his last delusion.

Hermann Goering's early days were as unusual as his later life. Born in Bavaria on 12 January 1893 to the wife of an eminent German diplomat, he was left to grow up with a family friend at the age of six weeks when his mother sailed to rejoin her husband in Haiti. His substitute father for three years was

"I have no conscience. Adolf Hitler is my conscience."

a rich medical man of Jewish descent who, when the Goerings returned to Germany, embarked on a 15-year affair with the young Hermann's mother.

As he grew, Goering showed an early interest in military uniforms and dressing up, a trait that was to resurface later in life. After graduating from a military academy he joined the Prussian army and was stationed in the disputed territory of Alsace when World War I broke out. Here he was hospitalised when he suffered a severe bout of rheumatism – an affliction that was to prove the making of him.

During his convalescence he was talked into joining the German air force and, after being refused once, flew as a friend's unauthorised observer.

HERMANN GOERING

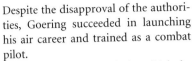
BELOW Goering
aged 14 showing
an early interest in
military uniforms and
dressing up

Despite the disapproval of the authorities, Goering succeeded in launching his air career and trained as a combat pilot.

After another setback in which he was wounded in the hip, he made his way steadily up through the ranks, regularly scoring air victories and decorations along the way. He was awarded the Iron Cross as well as the Pour le Mérite medal – the coveted Blue Max – and by the end of the war he had been credited with 22 kills.

Shortly after receiving the Blue Max, the air ace received further reward with the command of the notorious Jagdgeschwader 1 unit, four air squadrons that enjoyed the nickname the Flying Circus and had previously been commanded by Manfred von Richthofen – the famous Red Baron. Goering had achieved the status of a hero.

Given his status, it was natural that the Nazi party should welcome Goering into its ranks, and he joined in 1922. Hitler soon gave him the kind of role he enjoyed – commanding the Sturmabteilung, better known to English readers as the SA, Stormtroopers or Brownshirts.

However they were known, they acted as the Nazi party's paramilitary arm and Goering revelled in the opportunity for action, as well as the new-found power, the role offered. 'I gave him a dishevelled rabble,' Hitler said later. 'In a very short time he had organised a

division of 11,000 men.'

Many of Goering's SA men were deployed to accompany Hitler as he attempted to seize power from the detested Weimar Republic government in the Beer Hall Putsch of 8 and 9 November 1923. The attempt failed and, while Hitler was arrested and later imprisoned for high treason – giving him the chance to write Mein Kampf – his trusted lieutenant Goering was shot in the leg.

Once again, an enforced stay in hospital marked an important turning point in Goering's life. This time, as he lay in a hospital in Innsbruck, to where he had been smuggled by his wife and accomplices, he was treated with morphine. In no time he was dependent on the drug, and it was an addiction that was to shape much of his behaviour for the rest of his life.

And the problems started almost immediately. On the run from Germany and needing to minister to his sick wife, Carin, Goering travelled to her native Sweden. There the morphine addiction manifested itself in violent, unpredictable behaviour and in September 1925, confined in a straitjacket, he was admitted to a mental hospital.

An amnesty was declared for the agitators of the Beer Hall Putsch in 1927, and on his release from hospital Goering returned to Germany. The Nazi party was reorganising and there was no place for him at the head of the SA. Instead, he found himself manoeu-

LEFT Goering, Hitler and Himmler

vring on a more orthodox political front after being elected as a deputy in the 1928 Reichstag parliamentary elections.

A key event in the Nazis' rise to power occurred on 27 February 1933, when an arson attack on the Reichstag building in Berlin resulted in decrees that effectively banned anti-Nazi newspa-

ABOVE Carinhall where Goering often visited

pers and permitted detention without trial. Despite the fact that a communist activist claimed responsibility, Goering was linked to the fire in many observers' eyes.

In fact, he was reported to have said, at a celebration to mark Hitler's birthday in 1942: 'The only man who really knows about the Reichstag is me, because I set it on fire!' This could have been yet another incidence of typical Goering braggadocio, or the morphine talking. In any case, he denied responsibility at his Nuremberg trial.

Meanwhile, Goering's political career had led him to being appointed

Minister of the Interior for Prussia, Commissioner of Aviation and Minister without Portfolio after Hitler's ascent to the Chancellorship. He it was who first established the Gestapo secret police, later to be agents of terror throughout Nazi Germany and beyond, in Prussia. He told them: 'Shoot first and inquire afterwards, and if you make mistakes, I will protect you.'

With fellow Nazi thugs Heinrich Himmler and Reinhard Heydrich, Goering set about silencing political opposition in brutal fashion, and set up the first concentration camps, where the Nazis' enemies were incarcerated.

March 1935 saw the real start of Goering's second career in the German air force with the establishment of the Luftwaffe under his control – in contravention of the terms of the Treaty of Versailles – and he continued to accumulate power. Given a free hand to implement a huge rearmament and taking the ministries of labour and agriculture under his wing, he amassed an enormous fortune – and was not reluctant to spend it.

Goering's criminal and eccentric behaviour was apparent to anyone who visited the extraordinary hunting lodge

he had built in Schorfheide Forest, near the Polish border in north-east

BELOW One of the first concentration camps

Germany. Named after his first wife, who had died in 1931, Carinhall was the scene of lavish hunting trips and entertainment on a massive scale, and of an enormous collection of art treasures stolen from all over Europe.

The master of Carinhall made sure he

was first in the queue for the art and other items plundered from the Jewish collections and museums of the continent. It is said 26,000 railway wagons full of looted treasures from France alone ended up in Germany, and Goering often visited Paris to choose which of them would adorn his hunting lodge or palace in Berlin. But he was not only putting priceless pieces of art and furniture on display to open-mouthed guests. He was also exhibiting himself.

Changing his clothes up to five times in an evening, Goering switched from outrageously styled military uniform complete with a mass of medals to medieval hunting dress, from red Roman-style toga fastened with a gold clasp to a fur coat likened by one visitor to that of a high-class prostitute.

This was the behaviour of a bloated egomaniac obsessed by the trappings of wealth and power, and one who happened to be clutching lethal weapons in his increasingly chubby hands. This was also a man who was rapidly losing his already tenuous grip on reality. Styling himself the Iron Knight, Goering once said: 'I am what I have always been – the last Renaissance man, if I may be allowed to say so.'

With the war under way, Goering's stewardship of the Luftwaffe was affected by his increasingly loose judgment. From the Nazis' point of view he made fatal error after fatal error, contributing in large measure to the eventual loss of the war.

His marshalship of the Battle of Britain in the summer of 1940 is a prime example. At exactly the point in the conflict when the RAF was at its weakest, having suffered heavy losses of aircraft and men, he turned the attention of the Luftwaffe away from the fighter aircraft and their bases to the intensive bombing of London. Although the bombing campaign inflicted a terrible toll on the people of the British capital, his misguided decision gave the RAF the breathing space to recover, regroup, rebuild and eventually claim victory.

Hitler's longed-for invasion of England, Operation Sealion, had depended on German air supremacy. When this was snatched away and the invasion abandoned, Goering's standing in the eyes of the Führer – the man who nominated him as his successor – was considerably diminished. And Goering continued to make mistakes.

'No enemy bomber can reach the Ruhr,' he had told his Luftwaffe forces in 1939. 'If one reaches the Ruhr, my name is not Goering. You may call me Meier.' Many Germans later did indeed refer to the Reichsmarschall des Grossdeutschen Reiches as Meier. His conviction that Germany's industrial heartland was safe from Allied bombers proved to another of his delusions as his precious Luftwaffe failed in its defensive duties. This was the man who had been handed a rank at the very top of Germany's fighting forces.

ABOVE A V-1 Flying Bomb

Then there was the failure in Goering's handling of the Luftwaffe in Stalingrad, where his promise to handsomely supply the encircled German forces proved to be a shallow one. The Soviets were thus able to win the day in a victory that led to their eventual slow advance on Berlin. It was no wonder that Hitler harboured an increasingly violent loathing of the man.

Goering was detached from the reality of contemporary air warfare, preferring

HERMANN GOERING

BELOW Detention report and mugshots of Hermann Goering

to believe that the World War I-style heroism he held so dear had the edge over technological advance. He wound down research programmes – delaying the introduction of the V-1 flying bomb and V-2 rocket in the process – and went so far as to conceal the truth of the Allied air forces' advance into German territory from his colleagues. His days were numbered.

As the Soviet army moved in on Berlin, Carinhall was destroyed and its treasures moved to safekeeping and

Goering's sanity diminished further. After bidding farewell to the Führer for the last time on 20 April 1945 he retreated to his Bavarian estate, where he received a missive from Hitler accepting that the war was lost and stating that he intended to commit suicide.

Goering, in his deluded state, believed Hitler was stepping aside and proposed that he take over the leadership immediately. Hitler, in turn, interpreted the proposal as treason and had Goering stripped of all titles and arrested. The

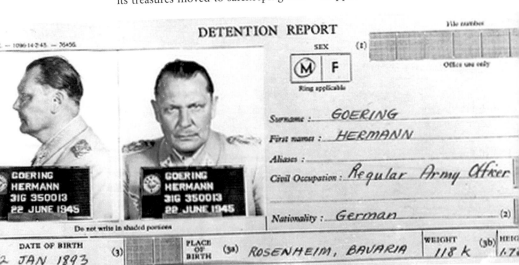

DETENTION REPORT

SEX (1)

Ⓜ F

Ring applicable

Surname : GOERING

First names : HERMANN

Aliases :

Civil Occupation : Regular Army Officer

Nationality : German (2)

GOERING HERMANN 3IG 350013 22 JUNE 1945

Do not write in shaded portions

DATE OF BIRTH	(3)	PLACE OF BIRTH	(3a)	ROSENHEIM, BAVARIA	WEIGHT	(3b)	HEIG
2 JAN 1893					118 k		1.7

former Reichsmarschall was captured by American troops on 9 May. From there, his road could lead to only one place: Nuremberg.

'The large and varied role of Goering was half-militarist and half-gangster,' prosecution lawyer Robert H Jackson told his trial. 'He stuck his pudgy finger in every pie.'

And there were many, many pies. Goering was not just responsible for the deaths of armed forces and civilians in his Luftwaffe operations; he had been a prime influence behind the Final Solution, ordering SS General Reinhard Heydrich to 'carry out all preparations with regard to … a general solution of the Jewish question'.

The newly slimline Goering, who had been obliged to endure cold turkey in prison to defeat his morphine addiction, defended himself vigorously. But he was found guilty of war crimes, crimes against humanity and conspiracy to wage a war of aggression, and

ABOVE Nuremberg trial

sentenced to hang.

Goering had one last trick up his sleeve. Two hours before he was due to climb the scaffold steps, he swallowed a cyanide capsule that had somehow been smuggled to him, and died in convulsions.

He had deprived his victims of justice thousands of times … now he had averted justice one last time.

Chapter 3

Hess -
The Deputy

RIGHT Rudolf Hess, 1935

The story of Rudolf Hess, Hitler's devoted deputy in the Nazi party and the man who transcribed the Führer's anti-Semitic manifesto Mein Kampf, is one of the most extraordinary of World War II. It is certainly one of the most controversial, hotly debated and, to some, unexplained.

The story could form the basis of a mystery thriller, a mini-series on political intrigue or a thesis on human stupidity. Indeed, it has inspired many a film, book and musical work and will doubtless continue to do so.

Why Hess flew alone from Germany to Scotland one day in 1941, apparently on a mission to propose peace between Britain and Germany, is still the subject of heated argument. Was it a true solo mission undertaken without the knowledge or approval of the Nazis, or was Hess following the orders of the Führer? Why was Hess incarcerated in isolation for year after year? Did he commit suicide in prison or was he murdered by the British secret service?

Whatever the truth, one fact is clear: the story of Hess's journey to notoriety is one that takes some explaining.

Rudolf Hess was born in Alexandria, Egypt on 26 April 1894 and grew up absorbing several different cultures and languages. His father, a wealthy businessman, made sure the family made regular trips home to Germany so his children would be familiar with the way of life of the Fatherland. The young

"*Hitler is simply pure reason incarnate.*"

Hess also learned English as he grew up in British-occupied Egypt – an accomplishment that stood him in good stead later in life.

When Hess was 14 the family returned to Germany where, despite the boy's interest in astronomy, he was encouraged to follow a business career. In 1914 the outbreak of war saw him joining an artillery regiment and he saw action at Verdun, Ypres and in the Carpathian Mountains. He suffered several wounds on the way to earning the Iron Cross, second class and transferred to the air force shortly before the end of the 1918 armistice ended the war. Crucially, the war did not end before Hess learned to fly aircraft.

He returned to the world of business

RUDOLF HESS

but, tiring of that life, resumed his studies – political science, geopolitics, history and geography – at the University of Munich. Here he met a man who was to have a huge influence on his thinking and that of Adolf Hitler, the geopolitician Karl Haushofer. His ideas emphasised self-sufficiency of the state, the notion that the state is greater than the individuals who form it and that the state needs lebensraum, or living space. They later helped to justify many of Nazi Germany's expansionist and repressive policies.

Not long after meeting Haushofer, Hess came under the influence of another charismatic speaker when he saw Hitler speaking at a Munich rally in May 1920. He fell hook, line and sinker for the future Führer's ideas and from that moment dedicated himself to serving him. He became one of the first members of the Nazi party and busied himself organising its activities in Bavaria.

It was natural that at some stage Hess should introduce Hitler to Haushofer, and the meeting duly took place in 1921. Hitler was profoundly affected by what he heard from the older man and plundered his theories to help in the formation of his own ideology. Haushofer became one of Hitler's closest advisers, but it was one of the ironies of the age that his wife and children were defined in 1935 as mischlinge (crossbreeds with partial 'Aryan' ancestry) under the Nuremberg Laws.

Hess was by now very close to the Nazi leader, and was at the head of a battalion of SA stormtroopers during the Beer Hall Putsch, Hitler's failed coup d'état of 1923. He was jailed in Landsberg Prison for his part in the attempt, and there his role became that of secretary to Hitler as the imprisoned Nazi leader dictated the words that were to become Mein Kampf.

Hitler's slow ascent to power recommenced after he was released from prison, and Hess's star was in the ascendant too. When, in early 1933, Hitler grabbed total control of Germany, Hess was named deputy to the Führer, and he was prominent in the spheres of diplomacy and lawmaking. He gained a reputation among European leaders for maintaining a cool, calm grip on affairs, something that could scarcely be expected of Nazi contemporaries like Goering and Himmler. Yet when it came to foreign affairs he found himself being to some extent pushed to one side as those contemporaries came to the fore.

Still, despite the fact that Hess was not involved in any of the plotting, scheming and manipulation that the other German leaders delighted in, he maintained his position of power and continued to serve Hitler. 'The party is Hitler and Hitler is Germany. Hitler is simply pure reason incarnate,' he continued to proclaim.

Then, in 1939, came the war. Britain's declaration of war against Germany fell

BELOW Hess in 1935

like a hammer blow on Hess. He had hoped that the two countries would find common cause against the Soviet Union and felt none of the thirst for victory over the old enemy that consumed most of Hitler's cronies. His heart was not in it.

Hess brooded for over a year then, on 10 May 1941, set off on the most

extraordinary flight of the war.

He had maintained the flying skills he had learned in the Great War, so when he boarded a Messerschmitt 110 equipped with auxiliary fuel tanks at the Bavarian city of Augsburg, he knew that he could reach his destination.

He could not have known, however, whether he would reach it without attracting the attentions of RAF fighter aircraft.

First, though, he was pursued by Luftwaffe pilots. He outstripped them and flew on, until he was spotted on British radar. Aircraft were scrambled to intercept him, but Hess succeeded in parachuting from his Me110, near the village of Eaglesham in Scotland, before the aircraft crashed.

Found by a farm worker who was brandishing his pitchfork, Hess said he was Hauptmann Alfred Horn and had a message of vital importance for the Duke of Hamilton. The Duke had met Karl Haushofer's son Albrecht during a visit to Berlin some years earlier, and is said to have had contacts with fascist groups in Britain.

Let a British intelligence service report take up the story. 'On Saturday night an Me110 had landed in Scotland and the airman, who had been injured, was taken to hospital,' it said. 'When he got there he asked if he could see the Duke of Hamilton as he had a message for him from Haushofer.

'On the nine o'clock news last night the German communiqué reported that

ABOVE
Messerschmitt Me
110D

Rudolf Hess had mysteriously disappeared in an aeroplane, and in today's papers it appears that the pilot of the aeroplane was none other than Rudolf Hess. I spoke to Mair of Edinburgh who rang me up this morning and told me that Hess was in the custody of the military at Maryhill Barracks, Glasgow and that the Duke of Hamilton had seen him for one hour on Sunday morning, after which he left to see the

Prime Minister.'

Hess, it seemed, was on a peace mission in which he hoped to involve the Duke of Hamilton and end the war between Britain and Germany. His mission was doomed to failure, however.

Prime Minister Winston Churchill ensured that Hess should get no further in his work by ordering him to be imprisoned for a short while in the

RUDOLF HESS

Tower of London, followed by a stay at a military hospital in Wales, where it is said he was treated for insanity.

Hess's proposals for peace were dismissed and he remained in custody for the rest of the war, until his 1945 trial in Nuremberg for crimes against peace and conspiracy to commit crimes.

Back in Germany, Hitler reacted to his deputy's actions by stripping him of all his offices and ordering that he be shot on sight if he ever returned to the country. Martin Bormann was announced as the Führer's new deputy.

Meanwhile, the question to which everyone on either side wanted an answer was: 'Why on earth had Hess taken his life in his hands to embark on a mission that he must have known would end in failure?'

Hess gave an answer on 10 June 1941, according to a book by his wife Ilse. First he summed up the puzzlement at his actions. 'My coming to England in this way is, as I realise, so unusual that nobody will easily understand it,' he said.

'I was confronted by a very hard

LEFT Hess In prison

BELOW Churchill insisted the death of Rudolf Hess was not a criminal case

decision. I do not think I could have arrived at my final choice unless I had continually kept before my eyes the vision of an endless line of children's coffins with weeping mothers behind them, both English and German, and another line of coffins with mourning children.'

Hess, it appeared, could not bear the thought of the continuation of the war between two nations he loved. The ultimate failure of his mission was, naturally, a devastating blow, but he told his trial at Nuremberg in 1946 that he had no regrets about that or about his devotion to Hitler.

'I was permitted to work for many years of my life under the greatest son whom my people have brought forth in its thousand-year history,' he said.

'Even if I could, I would not want to erase this period of time from my existence.

'I am happy to know that I have done my duty, to my people, my duty as a German, as a National Socialist, as a loyal follower of the Führer. I do not regret anything. If I were to begin all over again, I would act just as I have acted, even if I knew that in the end I should meet a fiery death at the stake.'

Sentenced to life imprisonment by the Nuremberg judges, Hess spent the rest of his days in Spandau Prison, in the west of Berlin. He was that institution's most celebrated occupant and, following the release of fellow Nazis Albert Speer and Baldur von Schirach in 1966, its only one.

In strict isolation and allowed severely limited visits from his family, his mental health is said to have deteriorated. British concerns over his harsh treatment in prison were dismissed by the Soviet Union, which was jointly responsible for his incarceration.

After more than 40 years in Spandau, Hess was found in a summerhouse, a length of electrical cord around his neck, on 17 August 1987. The ruling of an autopsy was that he had committed suicide by asphyxiation.

Questions remain to be answered definitively. Was Hess acting alone, or on the orders of Hitler? Was he mentally ill? Did he commit suicide or was he murdered?

Claims were made during the war, and have been repeated ever since, that Hess's mission was not the solo initiative it appeared to be. Hitler, it was claimed, was as anxious to sign a treaty with Britain as Hess himself and sent his deputy, who spoke excellent English and was trusted abroad, to seek sympathisers who would help to promote the idea. Little evidence to support this claim has been forthcoming.

On the question of Hess's mental state, Churchill seemed to have no doubts. 'He was a medical and not a criminal case, and should be so regarded,' he wrote in his war memoir The Grand Alliance. Hermann Goering was also of the opinion that Hess had mental problems. 'Hess was slightly off balance for as long as I can recall,' he told the psychiatrist Leon Goldensohn in 1946.

Hess's son, Wolf Rüdiger, was convinced that his father was murdered in Spandau. Indeed, the man in charge of

LEFT The grave of Rudolf Hess

a second autopsy is said to have stated that he could not be sure no one else was involved in his death, and a book published in 2008 claimed that Hess was murdered by British secret agents. How on earth, it is often asked, could a frail 93-year-old man have the strength to lift his arms above his head and strangle himself?

It is probable that these and other questions will never be answered to the satisfaction of the conspiracy theorists. The mystery of Rudolf Hess's madcap mission will continue to baffle.

Chapter 4

Himmler -
The Executioner

RIGHT Heinrich
Himmler, 1938

It may sound absurd to say Heinrich Himmler was probably the most feared man in Nazi Germany, given the presence of a monster like Hitler as head of state, but a brief study of the man and his deeds will give credence to the statement.

Himmler was, after all, responsible for countless crimes against humanity as the head of the SS and the Waffen-SS paramilitary organisations. He was also an enthusiastic prime mover behind the mass extermination of Jews and other peoples in the Holocaust. He was recently named the greatest mass murderer of all time by the German magazine Der Spiegel, and when you consider what competition he had for that title you begin to appreciate how deadly Himmler was.

Cruel taskmaster to those below him and unblinking creator of atrocity after atrocity, while cringingly docile to his master, Himmler was the epitome of the callous Nazi bent on the coolly efficient elimination of those he considered inferior.

'In my eyes, Himmler was worse than Hitler,' Nazi official Erich von dem Bach-Zelewski told a psychiatrist in 1946. 'The assassination attempt [targeting Hitler] should have been directed against Himmler in the first place.'

Himmler was born in Munich on 7 October 1900 and was named after his godfather, Prince Heinrich of Bavaria.

*"The best political weapon
is the weapon of terror.
Cruelty commands respect."*

An early indicator to his later behaviour came at school, where his father, the principal (and a man who called his son 'a born criminal'), ordered him to spy on other pupils.

Another formative influence at that school was fellow pupil Karl Gebhardt, who would later become Himmler's personal doctor and, more chillingly, carry out surgical experiments on inmates of the Auschwitz and Ravensbrück concentration camps.

The outbreak of war in 1914 saw the teenage Himmler showing a great interest in its events, and he trained with the Bavarian cadet corps. In 1918 he was able to start training with a reserve regiment but history records that he struggled to cope even before he had a

HEINRICH HIMMLER

RIGHT Himmler as
a child

BELOW Munich Beer
Hall Putsch of 1923

chance to fight. The war soon ended anyway, and Himmler had to be content with helping the Freikorps volunteer army to defeat the short-lived Bavarian Soviet Republic.

His desire for military action of any kind remained, but Himmler completed his studies while joining a paramilitary group and meeting Ernst Röhm, later to become a co-founder of the Sturmabteilung, better known as the SA. Röhm was to figure prominently in Himmler's later life.

It was at Röhm's side, as a standard bearer, that he took part in the Munich Beer Hall Putsch of 1923, the attempted coup d'état that landed Hitler in jail. Himmler escaped detention and turned for a while to poultry farming – a failure, like many aspects of his early life – but his involvement with the Nazi party grew.

He worked as propaganda leader of the party from 1925 to 1930 and in 1929 was appointed head of Hitler's personal Schutzstaffel bodyguard, known to the world as the SS. The organisation, at that time a small body of black-shirted men, was coming out from under the SA's wing to become autonomous. It was to grow enormously and, under Himmler's direction, become the instrument of his most deadly work.

Elected to the Reichstag in 1930, he set about increasing the influence and manpower of the SS, a task in which he achieved staggering success – the number of men under his control had reached 52,000 by 1933.

Despite the rapid rise in membership, it was no easy task to be accepted into the SS. Every would-be member was scrutinised closely to ensure he fitted the 'Aryan' requirements demanded by the Nazi ideology. It was like a nursery gardener trying to reproduce a good, old strain which had been adulterated and debased, said Himmler. 'We started from the principles of plant selection and then proceeded quite unashamedly to weed out the men whom we did not think we could use for the build-up of the SS.'

Thus, by ensuring that their breeding stock was 'pure', the Nazis aimed to produce what they regarded as the true Aryan master race. That Himmler himself did not much resemble the Aryan ideal was not thought important.

This was a man who had great faith in astrology, in the power of heavenly bodies to shape man's destiny, and one who had many romantic beliefs and ideals based on legends and myths. His SS men formed a 20th century

BELOW Himmler and Rohm

ABOVE Himmler was clear in his views on anti-Semitism

equivalent of the Teutonic Knights – a crusading military order of the Middle Ages – and ceremonies were often held at night in castles lit by flaming torches. Like the mythical King Arthur, he would preside over tables of 12 men, and he urged his officers to

consume only leeks and mineral water at breakfast.

This was also a man who set up the Lebensborn programme, which provided aid to the wives of SS men and to unmarried mothers. He supported the idea of single women, as long as they were racially 'pure', breeding with SS members, and he told his forces in 1939 that all women, single or married, should get themselves impregnated by good Nordic men about to go off to war.

Himmler was quite clear about his attitude to Jewish people: they were unclean. 'Anti-Semitism is exactly the same as delousing,' he is reported as saying. 'Getting rid of lice is not a question of ideology, it is a matter of cleanliness. In just this same way, anti-Semitism for us has not been a question of ideology but a matter of cleanliness.'

And he was equally straightforward in his views on how to wield power most effectively. 'The best political weapon is the weapon of terror,' he is reported to have said. 'Cruelty commands respect. Men may hate us. But we don't ask for their love; only for their fear.'

At the same time as he was strengthening his SS power base, Himmler was organising the Security Service with Reinhard Heydrich and accumulating power in other areas. The appointments came in a dizzying rush: President of Munich police, Commander of the political police in Bavaria; then of all political police units outside Prussia; then, finally, head of the Prussian police

in 1934. At the same time, Himmler became the commander of the Prussian Gestapo.

At this point, Ernst Röhm loomed large in his life again. The SA com-

BELOW Himmler visiting Dachau

mander was regarded by Himmler, Hermann Goering and others as a threat to the party leadership, and perhaps with good reason. Röhm was eager to merge the German army into the SA, with him at its head, and he was suspected of preparing a coup.

Once Hitler had been persuaded by Himmler and his cronies that Röhm represented a real threat, the latter's time was up. The so-called Night of the Long Knives – actually three nights – eliminated the SA leadership, with Röhm and many others being murdered. With the SA leadership out of the way, Himmler's power base at the head of the SS was assured.

He had been active in many spheres before the Night of the Long Knives, and one of them was the establishment of the first concentration camps. At first, the camps were used for the internment of political enemies of the

Nazis, as was seen at the first of its kind – Dachau, set up in 1933. Soon, however, Himmler was using the camps to imprison much broader sections of German society.

His conviction that the creation of a Nordic super-race was within the grasp of the Nazis, shown in his SS recruitment policy, was manifested in the camps. 'There is no more living proof of hereditary and racial laws than in a concentration camp,' he said in 1937. 'You find there hydrocephalics, squinters, deformed individuals, semi-Jews: a considerable number of inferior people.'

Himmler vowed to dedicate himself to 'the struggle for the extermination of any sub-humans, all over the world, who are in league against Germany, which is the nucleus of the Nordic race; against Germany, nucleus of the German nation; against Germany the custodian of human culture: they mean the existence or non-existence of the white man; and we guide his destiny.'

They were chilling words, and they were to prefigure the annihilation of millions of humans in the coming Holocaust, with the SS acting as the executioners. When, in 1941, it was decided that all the Jews of Europe must be exterminated, Himmler proved a supremely efficient executor of the command.

At first, the mass murders were carried out by the Einsatzgruppen, mobile death squads of SS men, who rounded up Jews and other groups in the territories of Poland and the Soviet Union over-run by the Nazis, and shot them in large numbers. The Einsatzgruppen did a good job, Himmler conceded, but the speed of extermination had to be accelerated and his men had to be spared the potentially traumatic act of shooting women and children in cold blood.

So the death camps were born. Mobile gas chambers were used to carry out the grisly task of killing dozens of victims at a time, but the work was carried out on an infinitely larger scale in the camps.

A logical extension of Himmler's beloved concentration camps, the extermination camps of western Poland were the scenes of slaughter on an unimaginable scale. At Auschwitz, Belzec, Chelmno, Majdanek, Sobibor and Treblinka, thousands of Jews, Slavs, Gypsies and other population groups poured into the camps and, having

met their fate clawing at the doors of the gas chambers in vain attempts to escape, never left. It is thought that up

BELOW Himmler before capture in 1945

to 3.5 million people were murdered at these sites.

In October 1943, Himmler stood up to address a secret meeting of the Nazi elite in the Polish city of Poznan. His intention was to explain what was happening as the Final Solution was carried out and its implications for the future of Germany. He was going to mention a 'very difficult subject', he told those assembled, but it was a subject that should never be discussed in public. 'I am talking about the "Jewish evacuation", the extermination of the Jewish people,' he continued.

'Most of you here know what it means

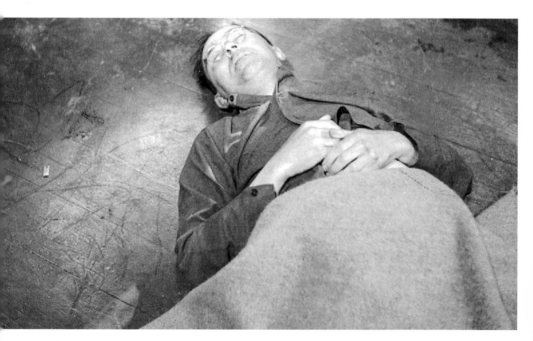

when 100 corpses lie next to each other, when there are 500 or when there are 1,000. To have endured this and at the same time to have remained a decent person – with exceptions due to human weakness – has made us tough, and is a glorious chapter that has not and will not be spoken of.

'Because we know how difficult it would be for us if we still had Jews as secret saboteurs, agitators and rabble rousers in every city, what with the bombings, with the burden and with the hardships of war. If the Jews were still part of the German nation, we would most likely arrive now at the state we were at in 1916 and 1917.'

Six million of those Jews, and perhaps a further six million other people, were killed as a result of Himmler's brutal efficiency. No one knows the true number.

As the war drew to its close, Himmler proved himself resourceful as well as cruel. Styling himself the provisional leader of Germany, he approached Allied forces with proposals for the Nazis' surrender and a peace pact, with the Allies joining his nation in an onslaught against the Soviet invaders. When Hitler heard of his deputy's

actions he called them the worst act of treachery he had ever encountered, and stripped Himmler of all his titles.

Himmler's entreaties to the Allies failed and, friendless, he wandered around Flensburg, near Germany's border with Denmark, having shaved off his distinctive moustache and adopted an eye patch. The rather pathetic disguise failed to prevent his arrest by British troops on 22 May 1945, and his true identity was revealed by fellow captives.

He was, of course, due to face charges of genocide at Nuremberg, along with his one-time friends at the head of the Nazi party, but he was too cunning – or cowardly – to face that fate. According to the diary of Corporal Harry Oughton Jones, one of the British troops charged with ensuring Himmler did not commit suicide in captivity, the SS commander laughed in the young soldier's face. Oughton Jones said: 'As we made to get him he just put his hand to his mouth and before we got to him he dropped dead on the bed.'

It was a rapid death due to cyanide poisoning from a suicide capsule, rather faster than those of the millions he condemned to the gas chambers.

Chapter 5

Doenitz -
The Admiral

RIGHT Karl Doenitz,
1943

There is no argument that Karl Doenitz was a brilliant naval strategist and an unswervingly loyal servant of his Führer and his country. There is much debate, however, over whether he was a callous war criminal who was fully aware of the horrors committed by his comrades in the name of the Nazi ideology he so eagerly embraced.

A career naval commander who became Grand Admiral of the Kriegsmarine (the German navy) in 1943 and who eventually succeeded Hitler as head of state, Doenitz became known for the lethally efficient 'wolf pack' tactics of his U-boats. He was also an enthusiastic Nazi and anti-Semite. But at his Nuremberg trial he vehemently denied knowledge of the atrocities being carried out in eastern Europe against Jews and other peoples.

Could someone who had the ear of the Führer and was so close to the highest level of the Nazi party really be so ignorant of that party's policies? He was capable of ordering his men not to attempt rescue of the victims of his U-boats' attacks, leaving them to drown. Was he not also capable of contemplating the systematic extermination of a people he despised?

Should Doenitz have been subject to a harsher sentence than the 10 years in prison the judges handed down at Nuremberg?

Karl Doenitz was born on 16

"*No attempt of any kind must be made at rescuing members of ships sunk.*"

September 1891 in the Berlin district of Grünau and showed an early inclination to lead the life of a sailor. He became a sea cadet in the Imperial German Navy at the age of 19 in 1910 and soon rose to the rank of midshipman.

Commissioned as an acting sublieutenant in 1913, he began World War I by serving on a cruiser, first in the Mediterranean and later taking on the Russian navy in the Black Sea. In 1916 he transferred to the section of the navy for which he showed most affection throughout his career, and in which he became an acknowledged master: submarines.

First he served as watch officer on one U-boat and then, in February 1918,

KARL DOENITZ

he took command of another. His second command, of a U-boat in the Mediterranean, came to an abrupt end when the vessel was sunk and Doenitz was taken prisoner by British forces. He was taken to Britain and remained as a prisoner of war in Sheffield until his release in the summer of 1919.

His career resumed on his return to Germany, first in the naval arm of the army and then in the navy itself. By this time he was enjoying the rank of Lieutenant and a growing reputation.

By 1928 Doenitz was serving in charge of torpedo boats and assuming the rank of Lieutenant-Commander, and by 1933 – the year Hitler took total control of Germany – he was a full Commander, in charge of a cruiser. His ascent continued to be rapid. September 1935 saw him promoted to Captain, with a U-boat flotilla under his command. In that same year, the Nazis changed the name of the state's seagoing forces to Kriegsmarine – War Navy.

Meanwhile, Doenitz was thinking deeply about the role of submarines in war and was formulating the policy for which he would become known. In direct opposition to the strategies adopted by all major navies of the time, he felt the submarine should play the major role in maritime conflict, while the part played by surface vessels should be limited. A major effort should be made to build up Germany's U-boat

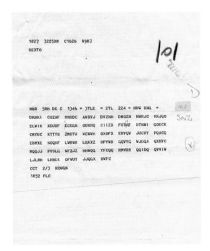

fleet, he felt, and he pressed for this to happen – despite the fact that such a move would be in direct contravention of the terms of the Treaty of Versailles signed at the end of World War I.

Doenitz's thinking was based on sound principles. The success of U-boat wolf pack tactics in World War I had been limited by a lack of suitable radio equipment, but by the mid-1930s

things were different. Ultra-high frequency radios were available and it was believed they could not be jammed. And they were supported by what Nazi Germany hoped would be a formidable weapon: the Enigma machine.

The Enigma electro-mechanical cipher machine could be used to send encrypted messages that, the Germans believed, could not be broken. In fact, by the time World War II broke out its secrets had been unravelled by Polish engineers and, despite the fact that increasingly sophisticated Enigma machines were developed, the Allies managed to keep abreast of the developments – just. The work of the British code-breakers of the Ultra programme in decrypting a vast number of German communications is sometimes credited with shortening the war by up to two years. Prime Minister Winston Churchill later said: 'It was thanks to Ultra that we won the war.'

But back in the 1930s, Doenitz had faith in his Enigma machines, and he was working tirelessly to develop his U-boat fleet and its Rudeltaktik – wolf pack tactics. Merchant shipping crossing the Atlantic with vital supplies for Britain was to be hunted down by

KARL DOENITZ

BELOW The battleship Scharnhorst

coordinated lines of U-boats strung out across the convoy routes. Once a convoy was located the torpedo-equipped pack would gather to carry out the kill.

RIGHT Doenitz in 1943

Another successful tactic was to be used to avoid the convoys' sonar detection equipment: attacks would be carried out under cover of the night from near the surface, or even at the surface.

Doenitz's plans met fierce opposition from established naval leaders, not least from Grand Admiral Eric Raeder, commander of the Kriegsmarine. But Doenitz's star was in the ascendant, and

in January 1939, eight months before Britain declared war on Germany, he was promoted to the rank of Commodore, taking command of the U-boat fleet.

In the early months and years of the war Doenitz continued to rise in rank, reaching the level of Vice Admiral in 1940. Although he was at first unable to put his wolf pack plan into full operation – the small number and type of U-boats at his disposal made it impossible – his U-boat crews nevertheless scored some impressive victories. Allied merchant shipping was forced to sail under escort from naval warships, and many a vessel was sunk.

But from the end of 1942, when Doenitz was finally able to put his Rudeltaktik into operation, the number of losses skyrocketed. The wolf packs became ruthless killers prowling the oceans for their victims and, despite the fact that the Allies were able to intercept and decode much of the Kriegsmarine's Enigma communication, Britain's supplies of fuel and other commodities were threatened. Doenitz was on the rise again.

In January 1943 Raeder resigned his post as Grand Admiral, and his natural successor was Doenitz. The newly installed Kriegsmarine chief continued to score victories but also suffered important losses among his fleet of surface warships – notably that of the battleships Scharnhorst and Tirpitz – and it was obvious that the tide of the war had long since turned against Germany.

Doenitz had always been steadfast in his expressions of loyalty to Hitler and espousal of Nazi ideology. Nevertheless, it was something of a surprise when, on 29 April 1945, in his last will and testament, the Führer named the master naval tactician as his successor as head of state, president and supreme commander of armed forces. The men who had stood ahead of him in line to succeed Hitler – Goering and Himmler – had incurred the Führer's wrath, and the way was clear for Doenitz to take control when Hitler committed suicide on 2 May.

ABOVE Doenitz with Hitler

rather than the rampaging Soviet forces. He authorised Colonel-General Alfred Jodl to sign the documents of unconditional surrender to the Allies, and the war ended on 8 May. The reign of Doenitz as head of state of Nazi Germany had lasted exactly 23 days.

At the Nuremberg trials he was found not guilty of crimes against peace and humanity and war crimes, but guilty of waging a war of aggression and crimes against the laws of war. He was sentenced to 10 years in Spandau Prison.

After his release in 1956, Doenitz lived quietly in a small village in northwest Germany, working on his memoirs and corresponding with historians. Unrepentant of his actions until the end, he died of a heart attack on 24 December 1980.

His funeral was attended not only by former colleagues in the Kriegsmarine but also by officers of the Royal Navy.

Karl Doenitz, first as commander of German's B-boats then as chief of all naval operations, was responsible for the deaths of many thousands of sailors on both sides and just as many merchant seamen. The loss of life during the Battle of the Atlantic between 1939 and 1945 was appalling: 30,000 sail-

Not that his new, exalted titles meant much. He knew Nazi Germany's end was near, and he devoted most of his energies to ensuring that his forces surrendered to American or British troops

ors on the German side, 36,200 Allied sailors and 36,000 merchant seamen. Then there was the loss of shipping and much of the supplies the merchant ships contained: the Allies lost 3,500 merchant vessels, totalling 14.5 million gross tons, and 175 warships.

Doenitz never tried to deny his responsibility for these terrible losses; to do so would have been foolish. And the charges arrayed against him were grave.

The charge of waging unrestricted submarine warfare – the sinking of merchant vessels without warning –

arose partly from orders he issued on 17 September 1942, after an American Liberator bomber attacked a U-boat. The fact that the U-boat crew were rescuing Allied sailors and troops and Italian prisoners of war at the time led Doenitz to proclaim: 'No attempt of any kind must be made at rescuing members of ships sunk, and this includes picking up persons in the water and putting them in lifeboats, righting capsized lifeboats, and handing over food and water.

'Rescue runs counter to the most primitive demands of warfare for the

BELOW Detention report and mugshots of Karl Doenitz

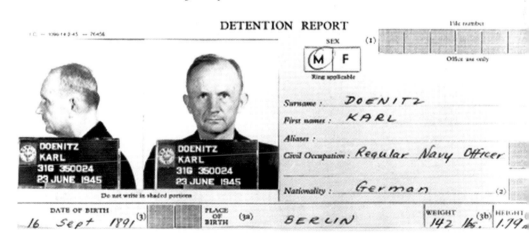

BELOW U-boat, U-534

destruction of enemy ships and crew. Be hard, remember that the enemy has no regard for women and children when he bombs German cities.'

At Nuremberg, Doenitz was found guilty, but the judges chose not to sentence him on that particular charge because the Allies were guilty of similar crimes. They cancelled each other out, in other words.

There were other charges – that he allowed a Hitler order condemning Allied commandos to summary execu-tion to remain in force, for example – but Doenitz was firm in his defence when it was put to him that he was part of the Nazi conspiracy to annihilate the Jews of Europe. He told the psy-chiatrist Leon Goldensohn: 'I accept responsibility for U-boat warfare from 1933 onwards, and of the entire navy from 1943 on, but to make me respon-sible for what happened to the Jews in Germany, or Russian soldiers on the eastern front – it is so ridiculous that all I can do is laugh.

'I read some time around 1938 of Jewish fines and some street actions against them. But I was too concerned with U-boats and the naval problems to be concerned about Jews.'

Doenitz was an anti-Semite, of that there is no doubt. He was fanatical in his adherence to Nazi ideology and his devotion to his Führer, and he is reported to have said in 1944: 'I would rather eat dirt than see my grandchildren grow up in the filthy, poisonous atmosphere of Jewry.'

Is it possible that a man who was so close to the planners and executors of the Final Solution, and who expressed such extreme views, could have known nothing of the genocide being committed in eastern Europe? Doenitz maintained his innocence until the end, and Goldensohn, who examined his mental state, thought he might have been sincere. 'I don't believe this man has any notion of what is going on in the world,' he wrote.

'He is acute, in no ways dull, but his mind seems to have blocked out the salient features of the trials thus far. He rejects the atrocities, the killing of millions of Jews, the barbarism of the SS, the entire criminal modus operandi of the Nazi party. He sees only that he was innocent of any crime, past or present, and that any attempt to incriminate him or any of the others on trial with him is political connivery.'

But if Doenitz was innocent of crimes on land, there is no doubting the effect of his lethal actions on the high seas. British wartime Prime Minister Winston Churchill said: 'The only thing I truly feared during the war was Doenitz and his U-boats.'

Chapter 6

Speer -
The Architect

RIGHT Albert Speer,
1946

Without Albert Speer's genius for organisation and dedicated work to ensure German manufacturing output reached the highest possible level, World War II would not have lasted as long as it did. His use of forced labour from millions interned in concentration camps and imported from conquered territories also helped the Nazi war machine to keep ticking over until the last days of the war.

But Speer, who began his career among the Nazis as an inspired architect, was unique among the war criminals who went on trial at Nuremberg. He was the only one who showed remorse for his crimes, and even those of other men. He admitted his guilt, wrote a memoir in which he condemned the actions of Hitler – the man who had promoted him to high office – and even claimed he had planned to assassinate the Führer.

Speer maintained he knew nothing of the horrors of the Holocaust – a claim that is disputed in some quarters – but expressed regret that he did nothing to stop them. He also said he disobeyed Hitler's orders that industrial sites be destroyed once the war was drawing to a close.

Despite Speer's apparent contrition, he spent 20 years in Spandau Prison for his crimes.

Albert Speer was destined to follow a career in architecture. Born into a

"*One seldom recognises the devil when he is putting his hand on your shoulder.*"

wealthy family on 19 March 1905 in Mannheim, south-west Germany, he was the son and grandson of architects. As a young man he was keen to study mathematics but was persuaded to follow the family tradition by his father.

He studied at the universities of Karlsruhe and Munich before finishing at the Berlin Institute of Technology, where he fell under the influence of Heinrich Tessenow, a renowned architect and urban planner whose simplified designs owed much to German national culture. Speer became Tessenow's assistant and presided over some of his classes while pursuing his own studies.

He was still a young man when, encouraged to attend a Nazi rally by

ALBERT SPEER

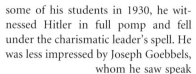

some of his students in 1930, he witnessed Hitler in full pomp and fell under the charismatic leader's spell. He was less impressed by Joseph Goebbels, whom he saw speak at another rally, but he had been sufficiently impressed by Hitler to apply to join the Nazi party in early 1931.

Speer can have had little idea at that point of the elevated status he would achieve within the party, especially as his first design commission merely involved the unpaid redecoration of a local Nazi leader's house. But his work was noticed, and when the party's headquarters in Berlin needed renovation he was recommended for the job. Again, his work met with an enthusiastic response.

In all probability thinking that was that as far as work for the party was concerned, Speer was pleasantly surprised when he was commissioned to renovate another building: Goebbels' Ministry of Propaganda. Soon after, in 1933, he saw the designs for the Nazis' May Day rally, to be held in Berlin, and insisted he could do better. The design that followed, with its use of enormous flags, was to form the template for many rallies to follow, and found favour with Hitler.

Speer's progress within the Nazi party began to accelerate. He was asked to provide designs for the party's Nuremberg 1933 rally, which Hitler approved, and this led to the young architect's appointment as Commissioner for the Artistic and Technical Presentation of Party Rallies and Demonstrations. But it was while he was working on another renovation project – that of the Chancellery in Berlin – that Speer began to form a close association with the Führer.

Hitler was greatly interested in progress at the Chancellery, and in Speer himself. The young man was rapidly drawn into Hitler's inner circle of advisers and it became clear he had become the man chosen to bring to reality the architectural elements of the Führer's grandiose visions of a new Germany. The two men became close, dining together and enthusiastically comparing ideas.

Later, at his Nuremberg trial, Speer would say: 'If Hitler had had any friends at all, I certainly would have been one of his close friends.'

By 1934 Speer had been placed at the head of the Chief Office for Construction, where he was in a position to realise Hitler's dreams. The grand project began with Speer's design of the gigantic parade grounds in Nuremberg – the Zeppelin Field – that can be seen to impressive effect in Triumph of the Will, Leni Riefenstahl's propaganda film telling the story of the week-long 1934 Nazi party congress.

The stadium featured a massive tribune – a raised platform from which speeches were made – based on but many times larger than the Pergamon Altar, a monumental construction built in the second century BC in Asia Minor. Capable of holding up to 340,000 people, the stadium was

enhanced by Speer's 'cathedral of light', the strategic placing of 130 anti-aircraft searchlights pointing their beams up into the night sky.

ABOVE Examining plans with Hitler

ABOVE The Zeppelin Field

Nazis, however, in Speer's design of the exterior of the Olympic Stadium, a rescue job he undertook when the original plans found disfavour with Hitler.

The following year saw the architect promoted to the rank of under-secretary of state, with the power to over-rule the city fathers of Berlin when it came to the planned rebuilding of the capital. And the designs Speer came up with ensured that he went down in architectural history.

At the heart of his plans was a three-mile north-south boulevard that Speer dubbed the Street of Magnificence. At the southern end would be a monstrous, 120-metre high triumphal arch capable of dwarfing the Arc de Triomphe of Paris and allowing a view of a massive assembly hall at the northern end. The Volkshalle – People's Hall – would accommodate 120,000 people and its dome would peak at 210 metres.

Those designs were never brought into being, but Speer's plan for a new Chancellery building in Berlin certainly was. Given an almost impossible schedule to complete a building of gargantuan scale, he brought the project in two days ahead of schedule.

His reputation for efficiency ensured

Speer came up with other plans to eclipse the Zeppelin Field. Nuremberg was scheduled to be the site of another parade ground capable of holding up to half a million people, but that design was never realised. Before the advent of World War II brought a similar end to many more of Speer's plans, however, he was responsible for other triumphs.

The 1936 Berlin Olympic Games were intended to showcase the superiority of Hitler's vaunted 'Aryan' super race, until the Führer was humiliated by the sight of a black American, Jesse Owens, vanquishing all comers in the sprints. The Games were a triumph for the

LEFT The Olympic Stadium

BELOW Speer after taking his new role as Minister or Arms

Speer would find plenty of work when the storm clouds of war broke over Germany. He failed to convince Hitler that work on the civic projects in Nuremberg and Berlin should cease completely in time of war, but he also oversaw the construction of buildings for the Nazi land and air forces. His organisational skills, however, ensured that he would soon be given a more prominent role – that of Minister of Armaments.

In his new position Speer made an immediate and deep impact. When he took office in 1942, Germany's industries were curiously inefficient in their production of the materials of war compared to those in Britain, for example. In addition, consumer goods were still being manufactured at

prewar levels, at the expense of munitions. Unlike their British counterparts, German women did not work in armaments factories.

Speer set about establishing more efficient working practices, ensuring

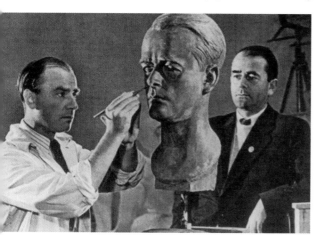

power over the war economy was centred on himself and switching factories that had produced consumer goods to the manufacture of armaments.

The effects of his genius for organisation were dramatic. In 1941 Germany produced the rather small number of 9,540 front-line machines and 4,900

tanks. By the end of 1944 those numbers had been multiplied many times, to 35,359 front-line machines and 17,300 tanks. Production of aircraft had been increased by 80 per cent and huge improvements had been made in the manufacture of U-boats. And those levels of production had been reached despite the nagging attentions of Allied bomber aircraft targeting the factories.

As time went on and Speer's reputation and power grew, he took on the title of Minister of Armaments and Production. He was now the principal architect of the whole of the German war economy, responsible for the building of roads and defences as well as weapons. In these projects his efficiency shone through just as it had in the munitions factories.

Speer's organisational abilities were clear, but he had also been helped in the achievement of his miracles by the use of slave labour. In violation of the Hague and Geneva Conventions, up to two million prisoners of war had been forced to work on his projects, and they were joined by another huge labour force: as many as seven and a half million foreign workers brought by force to Germany.

There is some evidence that Speer disliked the use of slave workers and the conditions they were forced to labour under. He would have preferred to use German women workers –Hitler was profoundly opposed to the women of the Fatherland working in factories – and took some steps to improve the lot of the foreign slaves and PoWs.

Nevertheless, thousands of these workers died as they helped to strengthen the Nazis' effectiveness in the business of war.

Meanwhile, Speer's relationship with Hitler was beginning to sour, and it took an unexpected turn in March 1945 when the Führer, faced with the collapse of his regime, ordered that indus-

LEFT PoWs working

ALBERT SPEER

trial installations in the paths of the advancing Allies should be destroyed. Speer persuaded Hitler to give him the power to carry out the order – and then disobeyed it.

When he was asked by American

forces after the war if he would tell them about the effects of Allied bombing on German war production, he readily agreed.

When Speer came to be judged for the part he had played in the Nazis' criminal activity, he was accused of crimes against peace, waging wars of aggression, war crimes and crimes against humanity. The chief American prosecutor at the Nuremberg trials, Robert H Jackson, told the judges: 'Speer, as Minister of Armaments and Production, joined in planning and executing the programme to dragoon prisoners of war and foreign workers into German war industries, which waxed in output while the labourers waned in starvation.'

Speer unhesitatingly accepted that he was as guilty as anyone else for the Third Reich's actions. He explained his position in his 1970 memoir Inside the Third Reich: 'In political life, there is a responsibility for a man's own sector. For that he is of course fully responsible.

'But beyond that there is a collective responsibility when he has been one of the leaders. Who else is to be held responsible for the course of events, if not the closest associates around the chief of state?'

He told the psychiatrist Leon Goldensohn in 1946 that he had tried to assassinate Hitler in 1945, a claim that drew scorn from other Nazis. But he insisted: 'I am not concerned with the jurisdiction of the court as Hess or others are. History will show the trials to be necessary.'

When the Nuremberg judges decreed that he should serve 20 years in prison, Speer remarked to the American psychologist Gustave Gilbert: 'Twenty years … well, that's fair enough. They couldn't have given me a lighter sentence, considering the facts, and I can't complain.' Years later, in 1977, he said the Nuremberg trials were to him 'an attempt to break through to a better world'.

And in his 1946 court testimony Speer talked about his knowledge of the anti-Semitic measures taken by Nazi Germany: 'I knew that the National Socialist Party was anti-Semitic, and I knew that the Jews were being evacuated from Germany.'

On his release from Spandau in 1966, Speer wrote and published his memoirs and made himself available for interviews. In September 1981, on his way to an appearance on the BBC's Newsnight programme in London, he collapsed and died.

The architect of the Nazi dream had served his time.

BELOW Speer at the Nuremberg Trials

Chapter 7

Eichmann -
The Bureaucrat of Murder

Adolf Eichmann never took a gun in his hands and shot a Jew. He never herded prisoners into a gas chamber, telling them they were going to be showered and rid of lice. His actions, however, condemned six million Jewish people and others to death.

Eichmann was the bureaucrat supreme, a master of planning, organisation and detail who took immense pleasure in the success of his schemes. Charged with the implementation of the Nazis' 'Final Solution to the Jewish question' – the eradication of the race from Europe – he oversaw every last detail of the Holocaust.

After the war Eichmann escaped jus-tice and fled to Argentina, where he lived under a false name and continued to raise a family. But justice was even-tually served when, after being cap-tured and delivered to Israel by secret agents – in an echo of the journeys endured by his victims – he faced trial for his crimes.

Described as the epitome of 'the fearsome, word-and-thought-defying banality of evil' by political theorist Hannah Arendt, Eichmann is still the only person ever to have been executed by the state of Israel.

Adolf Eichmann was born on 19 March 1906 near Cologne but moved to the town of Linz in Austria – the hometown of a man he was to serve faithfully in later life, Adolf Hitler –

> *" If we had killed 10.3 million Jews, then I would be satisfied and would say, good, we annihilated an enemy. "*

when he was eight. He failed at his engineering studies and worked at a succession of jobs before finding steady work as a salesman for a subsidiary of Standard Oil.

Eichmann was 26 when, encouraged by a friend, he joined the Austrian Nazi party and the Schutzstaffel (SS) in 1932, going on to gain early experience of life in a concentration camp as an SS squad leader at Dachau. The job proved not to his liking, however, and he was relieved when his request was approved for a transfer to the SD, the SS security service that was the province of Reinhard Heydrich.

At first assigned to a small office concerned with the activities of freemasons (one of the groups about which

the Nazis were particularly suspicious), Eichmann then transferred to the SD's Jewish section in Berlin. Here he was in his element, launching into a career that would see him maintain a deep interest in the Jews.

Eichmann took his job seriously as he rose steadily up through the ranks of the SS. He studied Jewish culture and Zionism, learned Hebrew and a little Yiddish and sat in on Jewish meetings. By becoming a specialist in Jewish matters he was doing his career prospects in the SS no harm, so it was little surprise when Heydrich and SS chief Heinrich Himmler appointed him to head up a museum of Jewish Affairs.

Another task assigned to him was the investigation of potential solutions to the question that vexed the Nazis most: what to do with the Jews? In 1937 he visited Palestine on a mission to investigate the possibility of mass emigration to the Middle East. Later, he even drew up plans for the forced repatriation of Germany's Jews to the Indian Ocean island of Madagascar. Like the Palestine idea, it was quietly dropped.

With the advent of the Anschluss – Germany's annexation and occupation of Austria in 1938 – Eichmann was assigned to Vienna, where he established the Nazis' Central Office for Jewish Emigration. By this time an SS First Lieutenant, he oversaw the running of concentration camps and the issuing of permits to Jews desperate to leave Austria. It is said nearly 100,000 Austrian Jews left the country, but not before they had eased the issuing of permits by agreeing to turn all their worldly possessions over to Eichmann's care. It was a highly profitable system for him and his masters.

Returning to Berlin in 1939, he was appointed head of Section IV-B4 of the RSHA, the Reich Main Security Office. By now enjoying the rank of an SS captain, Eichmann was henceforth responsible for the implementation of policy concerning the Jews of Germany and its occupied territories. Albeit from behind a desk, he had become one of the Nazis' most powerful men and was in place to implement the Final Solution.

Heydrich told Eichmann as early as the autumn of 1941 that the Jews of Europe were to be wiped out. In an interview with Israeli police much later, Eichmann recalled: 'The war with the Soviet Union began in June 1941, I think. And I believe it was two months later, or maybe three, that Heydrich sent for me. I reported.

'He said to me: "The Führer has ordered physical extermination." These were his words. And as though wanting to test their effect on me, he made a long pause, which was not at all his way. I can still remember that.

'In the first moment, I didn't grasp the implications, because he chose his words so carefully. But then I understood. I didn't say anything, what could I say? Because I'd never thought of a ... of such a thing, of that sort of violent solution.'

But Eichmann was definitely the man for the job. The genocide policy was set in stone at the Wannsee Conference the following January, and Obersturmbannführer (Lieutenant-Colonel) Eichmann was there in the capacity of recording secretary, ensuring that the spirit and the letter of the decree would be observed.

LEFT The SS insignia

ADOLF EICHMANN

BELOW Hungarian woman with children on the way to the gas chamber at Auschwitz-Birkenau

The full fury of the Nazis' extermination policy was now unleashed. First the Einsatzgruppen killing squads carried out their deadly work in the Soviet Union, keeping detailed records of their daily death tolls, as demanded by Eichmann.

In Minsk he watched as groups of Jews were shot and then, at Lvov, he witnessed the aftermath of a mass execution. At his trial in 1961 he told the shocked court that the ditch into which the victims had fallen had been covered over, but blood was shooting out of the ground 'like a geyser' under the pressure of gases released by the corpses.

Scenes like this were too much for SS chief Himmler, who ordered that his troops be spared this dirty work. Instead, the Jews were to be exterminated in the gas chambers of the death camps. Eichmann, in his guise as Transport Administrator of the Final Solution, did not stint in his work as Jews were transported by train from all over Europe to the camps in the east.

There they met their grisly fate. The commandant of the Auschwitz death camp, the infi-

BELOW Hungarian woman with children on the way to the gas chamber at Auschwitz-Birkenau

nitely cruel Rudolf Hoess, said in an affidavit at his Nuremberg trial that improvements were made to the killing machine following the experience of another camp, Treblinka. 'At Treblinka the victims almost always knew that they were to be exterminated and at Auschwitz we tried to fool the victims into thinking that they were to go through a delousing process,' he said.

'Of course, frequently they realised our true intentions and we sometimes had riots and difficulties due to that fact. Very frequently women would hide their children under their clothes,

ABOVE Killing of Jews at Ivangorod, Ukraine, 1942. A woman is attempting to protect a child with her own body just before they are fired on with rifles at close range

but of course when we found them we would send the children in to be exterminated.'

Hoess went on to explain how to murder up to 10,000 people within 24 hours. 'Technically it wasn't so hard,' he said. 'It would not have been hard to exterminate even greater numbers. The killing itself took the least time. You could dispose of 2,000 head in half and hour, but it was the burning that took the time.

'The killing was easy. You didn't even need guards to drive them into the chambers; they just went in expecting to take showers and, instead of water, we turned on poison gas. The whole thing went very quickly.'

This kind of clinical efficiency in the business of genocide was demanded by Eichmann, who took delight in the ever-mounting numbers of killings as evidence of a job well done. He travelled throughout the territories occupied by the Nazis, chivvying and cajoling the

LEFT A map of Auschwitz deportation

LEFT The main
entrance to
extermination camp
Auschwitz-Birkenau

SS executioners to ever greater death tolls. It was a job at which he, ever the perfectionist and stickler for detail, excelled, and by the summer of 1944 he was able to report to Himmler that four million Jews had been killed in the extermination camps and another two million by mobile death units.

Such was Eichmann's enthusiasm for the task in hand that he disobeyed Himmler's instructions to cease the deportation of Jews from Hungary as the Red Army closed in on Budapest towards the end of 1944. He oversaw the rounding up of another 50,000 Hungarian Jews, whom he sent on a murderous eight-day march to Austria. The job had to be finished to his satisfaction.

The end of Eichmann's work, and of the war, was at hand. In May 1945 he was arrested and interned by American troops, giving his name as Otto Eckmann, but in early 1946 he managed to escape and hide out in a hamlet on Lüneberg Heath in northern Germany. Here he bided his time until 1950, when he made his way first to Italy and then, under the name of Ricardo Klement, to Argentina. It is claimed by some that he was aided in

ADOLF EICHMANN

his escape from Europe by a clandestine organisation of former SS men.

Eichmann lived in Buenos Aires, eking out a living with various jobs and succeeding in bringing his wife and three sons to live with him. He even managed to add another son to the family in 1955. But while he had changed his name to Ricardo Klement, he failed to change those of his family. It was a crucial error.

Mossad, the Israeli intelligence agency, came to hear of people called Eichmann living in Buenos Aires and the net began to close in. On 11 May

1960 Adolf Eichmann was bundled into a car by Mossad and Shin Bet (security service) agents and, after being drugged so that he appeared drunk, was flown to Israel on an El Al aircraft.

The trial that was to lead to Eichmann's execution started in Jerusalem in April 1961 and finished 14 weeks later, having heard from 100 prosecution witnesses. They included 90 survivors of Nazi concentration camps and, importantly, former American naval officer Michael A Musmanno, who had questioned Nazi air supremo Hermann Goering at Nuremberg. Goering, said Musmanno, 'made it very clear that Eichmann was the man to determine in what order, in what countries, the Jews were to die.'

Chief prosecutor Gideon Hausner produced evidence in which Eichmann

was quoted as saying in 1945: 'I will leap into my grave laughing, because the feeling that I have five million human beings on my conscience is for me a source of extraordinary satisfaction.' Eichmann told Hausner that he was referring only to 'enemies of the Reich'.

And he was just obeying orders in organising genocide, he told the court. 'Why me?' he pleaded. 'Why not the local policemen, thousands of them? They would have been shot if they had refused to round up the Jews for the death camps. Why not hang them for not wanting to be shot? Why me? Everybody killed the Jews.'

The 'just following orders' defence had a familiar ring – it had been trotted out by defendants at the Nuremberg trials – and the Israeli judges were not convinced by it. Hardly any witnesses for the defence, all former high-ranking Nazis who sent depositions to the court, supported Eichmann's line of defence.

He was found guilty of crimes against humanity and against the Jewish people, war crimes and membership of an illegal organisation, and was sentenced to death. In the only execution ever carried out by the state of Israel, Eichmann was hanged at Ramla Prison, on 31 May 1962.

Ever the meticulous bureaucrat, Eichmann was once quoted as saying: 'Whether they were bank directors or mental cases, the people who were loaded on those trains meant nothing to me. It was really none of my business.' He was only doing his job.

BELOW Adolf Eichmann was found guilty and sentenced to death

Chapter 8

Bormann -
The Secretary

RIGHT Martin
Bormann, 1934

The top echelons of the Nazi party clustered around Adolf Hitler were riven by infighting, intrigue and political manoeuvring as military men, propaganda chiefs, bureaucrats and ideologues jostled to seek the Führer's favours. And at the top of them all, sitting quietly alongside Hitler, working in mysterious ways and pulling the strings to make his puppet comrades dance, was Martin Bormann.

Bormann, dubbed the Brown Eminence, was the master of subtle chicanery, a man who let nothing and no one stand in his way on his route to the very top of the Nazi pile. He controlled every communication route to the Führer; he controlled who could talk to Hitler; he even controlled the man himself. Some say he wielded more power than the man who relied on him so much. And he was utterly despised by those who lusted after power. 'Even among so many ruthless men, he stood out by his brutality and coarseness,' said the Nazi architect Albert Speer.

A vicious anti-Semite and a callous discarder of human lives, Bormann was at Hitler's side until the very end. Then he disappeared.

What became of him after he escaped from the Berlin bunker has been disputed ever since. Perhaps he died in the attempt. Maybe he lived out the rest of his life in South America. The argument rumbles on.

" Unfortunately this earth is not a fairyland but a struggle for life, perfectly natural and therefore extremely harsh. "

Bormann was born into a Lutheran family on 17 June 1900 in the Prussian town of Wegeleben. He did not show much inclination for school, preferring to drop out and try his hand at farm work. He served as a cannoneer in an artillery regiment at the end of World War I, without seeing active service.

After the war he joined a rightist Freikorps, fighting against the alleged wartime perpetrators of what was seen as the communist betrayal of Germany. It was here that Bormann learned the trades of assassin and bully, and the knowledge did not go to waste. In 1924 he was convicted of assisting Rudolf Hoess (later to command the Auschwitz death camp and not to be confused with Rudolf Hess) in the

murder of a man they believed had betrayed a fellow Freikorps member. He served a year in prison.

Bormann, once free, did not lose much time in joining the Nazis, becoming the party's press officer and then business manager in Thuringia. His rise thereafter was rapid: he was attached to the Sturmabteilung (SA) Supreme Command from 1928 and in 1933 became a Nazi Reichsleiter (Reich leader) – the highest party rank attainable save that of Führer. That year also saw him elected to the Reichstag.

He served in the office of Hitler's deputy, Rudolf Hess, as Chief of Cabinet from 1933 until 1941. It was in this position, acting as Hess's personal secretary and right-hand man, that Bormann sharpened the skills that would take him quietly to the top, earning Hitler's trust through his thorough efficiency, hard work and sinister diplomacy.

He it was who managed Hitler's finances and set up and ran the so-called Adolf Hitler Endowment Fund of German Industry – a scam that saw industrialists' gifts lining the pockets of leading Nazis. He it was, too, who commissioned the hugely expensive building of the Eagle's Nest, a mountain-top chalet above the town of Berchtesgaden, as a 50th birthday present for the Führer.

Many a party member underestimated Bormann's strengths and his determination to achieve ultimate power through sheer, uncomplaining persistence; they saw only his weaknesses. A small, squat, unprepossessing man with coarse manners and habits, Bormann seemed to lack the sophistication necessary to climb to the top. But all the while he was planning, making himself indispensable and awaiting his chance.

Albert Speer, writing in his memoir Inside the Third Reich, published in 1970, provided a telling insight into Bormann's character and methods. 'Most of the powerful men under Hitler

watched each other jealously like pretenders to the throne', he wrote. There were struggles for position among Goebbels, Goering, Alfred Rosenberg, Robert Ley, Himmler, Joachim von Ribbentrop and Hess. 'But none of them recognised a threat in the shape of trusty Bormann.

'He had succeeded in representing himself as insignificant while imperceptibly building up his bastions. Even among so many ruthless men, he stood out by his brutality and coarseness.

'He had no culture, which might have put some restraints on him, and in every case he carried out whatever Hitler had ordered or what he himself had gathered from Hitler's hints. A

MARTIN BORMANN

Bormann was a fanatical Nazi who did all he could to further the party's role in the Kirchenkampf – the 'struggle of the churches'. Hitler was keen to delay the Nazis' battle against the Christian churches until after the war, but Bormann waged the war nonetheless. 'National Socialism and Christianity are irreconcilable,' he is quoted as saying.

ABOVE Bormann (directly to Hitler's left) in Paris, June 1940

subordinate by nature, he treated his own subordinates as if he were dealing with cows and oxen.'

Bormann's big chance came when, in May 1941, Hess made his extraordinary flight to Scotland, hoping to make peace with Britain. Hess's position became vacant and Bormann was crowned Head of the Party Chancellery. Closer than ever to Hitler, he was now in a position to undermine his political rivals and conduct his intrigues from on high.

His rivals within the party were not the only ones who suffered, of course.

Meanwhile, he was busy consolidating his position, taking control of Hitler's diary, his paperwork and even his personal finances. He fought, quietly as ever, to strengthen the party's position against the SS and the Army. He held back the careers of figures like Goebbels, Himmler, Goering and Speer. 'Bormann's influence on Hitler was a national disaster,' said Speer.

He came to control aspects of policy, legislation, security and appointments of personnel. He even delved into the workings of the Wehrmacht, encouraging young army officers to spy on their superiors and report on their political leanings.

Following the party line to the letter, Bormann advocated the strictest adherence to policy in the matter of the so-called enemies of Germany – the Jews, the Slavs of eastern Europe, the gypsies and so on. He wrote in 1942: 'The Slavs are to work for us. Insofar as we do not need them, they may die.

'Therefore, compulsory vaccination and German health service are superfluous. The fertility of the Slavs is undesirable. They may use contraceptives or practise abortion, the more the better.'

It was not only fertility that was undesirable, according to Bormann; so too was education. 'Education is dangerous,' he claimed. 'It is enough if they can count up to one hundred. At best an education which produces useful coolies for us is admissible. Every educated person is a future enemy.'

It was Bormann who signed the decrees prescribing the use of 'ruthless

LEFT Bormann (behind and to Hitler's right) on the Old Bridge, Maribor, April 1941

force' in the 'special camps of the East' to deal with the Jewish Question and giving Adolf Eichmann absolute power to deal with the Jews.

By 1943, Hitler viewed Bormann as completely trustworthy and indispensable – he called him 'my most loyal Party comrade' – and the latter was ready to exploit still further his unique position. He controlled access to the Führer, denying meetings to the likes of Goebbels, Himmler and Goering; he took care of every administrative detail; he navigated Hitler down the paths of policy that he, Bormann, had chosen.

He was effectively Hitler's deputy, but in some ways he was even more powerful than the Führer himself. By the time the war was approaching the endgame Goering and Himmler were out of the way –thanks in large part to Bormann's scheming – and he was at Hitler's side in the final days in the bunker.

On 28 April 1945, with the Battle of Berlin raging in the streets above, he wired Grand Admiral Karl Doenitz: 'Situation very serious. Those ordered to rescue the Führer are keeping silent. Disloyalty seems to gain the upper hand everywhere. Reichskanzlei [the Chancellery] a heap of rubble.'

The following day he was one of those who witnessed the marriage of Hitler and Eva Braun, and signed the Führer's last will and testament.

On 30 April Hitler and Braun committed suicide, with Bormann still at their sides. He was now officially Party Minister, meaning he was the de facto General Secretary of the Nazi party, and Goebbels was in position as the head of government. Goebbels in turn killed himself on 1 May, but by that time Bormann had left the bunker on a mission to break through the lines of the Red Army and save himself.

Bormann was not alone in his breakthrough attempt; with him were others who had stayed in the bunker until the end: an SS doctor called Ludwig Stumpfegger, Hitler Youth leader Artur Axmann and Hans Baur, who was the Führer's pilot, formed part of one of the few groups that tried to sneak out of Berlin.

What happened next is the subject of much debate. The mysterious Martin Bormann, Brown Eminence of the Nazis, continued to create mystery.

According to one version, Bormann's group first attempted to cross the Weidendammer Bridge over the River

Daily Mirror

Wednesday, May 2, 1945
No. 12,906   ONE PENNY
Registered at G.P.O. as a Newspaper.

"GERMANY WILL BATTLE ON"

HITLER DEAD

Killed in Berlin, says new Fuehrer, Admiral Doenitz

HITLER was killed in action yesterday afternoon, according to a broadcast from Hamburg at 10.30 last night.

His successor is Rear-Admiral Doenitz, the C.-in-C. of the German Navy, who made the announcement himself.

Doenitz said: "The Fuehrer has fallen at his command post in Berlin. He fell for Germany."

Adolf Hitler, leader of the Nazi Reich since January 30, 1933, the world's chief criminal, now dead at the age of fifty-six.

This is Doenitz

Admiral Doenitz, who directed the U-boat war, and who now styles himself Head of the Nazi Reich

"MY FIRST TASK," SAID DOENITZ, "IS TO SAVE THE GERMAN PEOPLE FROM DESTRUCTION BY BOLSHEVISM. IF ONLY FOR THIS TASK THE STRUGGLE WILL CONTINUE.

"Give me your confidence. Do your duty. Keep order. Only in this way shall we be able to prevent collapse.

The German announcement came just as the House of Commons rose.

After a roll of drums, Hamburg radio said :

"It is reported from the Fuehrer's headquarters that our Fuehrer, Adolf Hitler, has fallen this afternoon at his command post in the Reich Chancellery fighting to the last breath against Bolshevism and for Germany.

"On April 30 the Fuehrer appointed Grand Admiral Doenitz as his successor.

"Our new Fuehrer will speak to the German people."

The last reference to Hitler was in yesterday's

Continued on Back Page

'Lay down your arms' —Graziani to his Army

MARSHAL GRAZIANI, commander of the German Army, who was captured by the Allies in Italy, said this over Rome radio last night:

"To Italian and German troops in Liguria, lay down your arms. For several days the German Supreme Command in Italy has not had any orders and its whereabouts are unknown. Under the circumstances, I took over the personal responsibility of signing unconditional surrender to the U.S. Command on April 29.

"Further resistance would not only be useless, but also dangerous for myself."

'Wait' is Churchill's tip to the Commons

MR. CHURCHILL told the Commons yesterday that he had no special statement to make about the war situation in Europe, but if information reached the Government this week—"as it might do"—he would tell the House.

It was not his idea that in formalities should be kept back "until the exact occupation of all the particular points."

DANES ARE TAKING OVER FROM THE GERMAN ARMY

THE Danes are taking control in their own country again. Danish police in full uniform are again patrolling the streets of several towns from which the Germans have withdrawn without incident.

This sensational news was reported by British United Press from Copenhagen, capital of Denmark, last night.

The Danish and German authorities, it was stated, are negotiating an agreement for the reinstatement of the Danish police all over the country.

Count Folke Bernadotte was yesterday reported to

have flown from Denmark with a German - Swedish agreement for the surrender of Nazi troops in both Denmark and Norway.

Danish underground sources reported that the movement of German troops from North to South Denmark had already begun.

Other sources believed that the Swedes had proposed—or the Huns had asked—that the German Army in Norway should go to Sweden to be disarmed there.

The Nazis want to get their troops into Sweden before

CIVIL SERVANTS ARE ASKING FOR HIGHER PAY

WAGE increases and reduced hours are urged in resolutions tabled for the two-day Annual Conference of the Society of Civil Servants next week in London.

A general stepping-up of annual increments is sought in one resolution from the Midlands, which also urges a five-day working week for the Civil Service when hostilities cease.

Snowfire Girls : MARGARET

Margaret is essentially a man's girl. She likes the drinks that men like; she appreciates good cooking and the finer points of most sports. And, as she is never separated from her Snowfire Beauty Makers, she is always good to look at.

Snowfire

BEAUTY MAKERS

For ever and a Date !

CREAM · POWDER · LIPSTICK

MARTIN BORMANN

Spree in a Tiger tank but it was hit by an anti-tank shell, with Bormann and Stumpfegger knocked over by the blast. Hitler's chauffeur, Erich Kempka, later said he was temporarily blinded by the explosion but nevertheless saw Bormann's corpse.

In another version of the story, the group eventually managed to cross the Spree and Bormann, Stumpfegger and Axmann were walking along railway lines when Axmann decided to make his own way in the opposite direction. Bumping into a Soviet patrol, he doubled back and saw, he later claimed, the bodies of Bormann and Stumpfegger near a railway switching yard, their faces illuminated by bright moonlight. Axmann succeeded in his escape attempt.

A Lieutenant-General of the Red Army, Konstantin Telegin, reportedly later recalled that Bormann's diary was brought to him by some of his men. 'As far as I can remember, it was found on the road when they were cleaning up the battle area,' he said. 'Naturally, we sent a recon group to the bridge, who searched the site of the breakthrough attempt. All they found were a few civilians. Bormann was not found.'

But in 1972, construction workers uncovered the remains of two men near a station in west Berlin. Dental checks seemed to confirm that one of the skeletons was indeed Bormann's, but the fact that the dentist who had attended him during the war was working from memory so many years later cast lingering doubt on the finding.

Of more use were a collarbone injury said to have befallen Bormann in 1939, traces of which were found on the skeleton, and the fact that fragments of glass were found in the jawbones of both men. Had they both committed suicide by cyanide capsule? It was certainly enough to convince the West German government, which declared Bormann dead.

It was not until 1998 that DNA tests were carried out on the skull thought to be Bormann's and compared to a relative. The test was positive: the skeleton found in 1972 was indeed that of the elusive Nazi, and the fact that Nuremberg judges had condemned him to death in absentia in 1946 seemed not to matter.

Or did it? Ever since his disappearance, sightings of Bormann had been reported here, there and everywhere. Security services and Nazi hunters throughout the world had puzzled over the enigma for decades.

First, in 1946, he was said to be in a monastery in northern Italy; his wife Gerda died of cancer in South Tyrol that same year, seeming to lend some kind of credence to the theory. Then it was said he was in Rome and had had plastic surgery to change his appearance; no, he was in Paraguay, Chile or Brazil; absolutely not, Bormann was in Argentina and, a millionaire, was living the high life in secret. The rumours multiplied with every passing year.

In the view of some people, the mystery of Martin Bormann has never been solved.

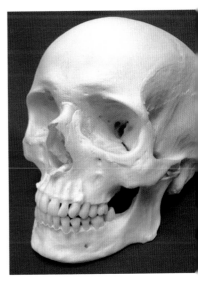

BELOW In 1998 DNA tests were carried out on the skull thought to be Bormann's

Chapter 9

Von Schirach -
The Corruptor of Youth

RIGHT Von Schirach, 1932

Baldur von Schirach was the cultured son of a theatre director who hymned Adolf Hitler's praises in verse while urging Germany's youth to strive for physical, not intellectual, perfection. He was an anti-Semite who deported thousands of Jews while pleading that they be treated better. He was the man who indoctrinated a generation of children with the toxic Nazi message of hate yet rejected that message later in life.

Von Schirach was a man of contrasts. But there were no contradictions when he was drilling, training and disciplining the enormous movement that was the Hitler Youth into becoming fighters for Hitler and his ideology. Neither were there any u-turns when he was driving thousands of Jews out of Vienna towards their uncertain fates in the ghettoes of eastern Europe.

It was said of him that he poisoned the minds of an entire generation – a generation that did not reason when it drove the mobile gas chambers or shot Jews in the back of the head; it simply carried out its orders.

When Von Schirach finished the prison term imposed on him for war crimes, he sat down and wrote a book called I Believed in Hitler. For years, the youth of Germany believed in Von Schirach.

Baldur Benedikt von Schirach had a privileged, cultured upbringing. He was born in Berlin on 9 May 1907

"*The striving for beauty is inborn among the Aryan.*"

to the theatre director and former cavalry officer Carl von Schirach and his American wife Emma Tillou. Descended through his mother from two men who had signed the United States Declaration of Independence, he grew up in comfortable circumstances with English as his first language. It was not until he was five that he learned to speak German.

Surrounded by music, literature and theatre from an early age, he did well at school and continued his studies, including German literature and folklore, art history and English, at the University of Munich. It was here, in 1925, that he joined a Nazi party that was then in its infancy.

Schirach's anti-Semitic views had

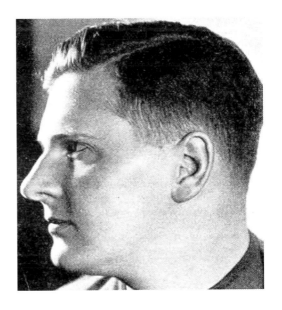

VON SCHIRACH

been influenced by reading American industrialist Henry Ford's The International Jew, as he was to tell his Nuremberg trial in 1946. 'We saw in Henry Ford the representative of success, also the exponent of a progressive social policy,' he said. 'In the poverty-stricken and wretched Germany of the time, youth looked towards America, and apart from the great benefactor, Herbert Hoover, it was Henry Ford who to us represented America.'

Giving up his studies to concentrate on youth work for the party, the young Schirach progressed rapidly and by 1929 had been named leader of the National Socialist German Students' League. He was proving to be a gifted propagandist and organiser, inspiring the Nazis' youth wing with messages of comradeship,

sacrifice, courage and honour. He was also becoming known for his poetry, in which he praised Hitler and all he stood for.

In 1931 Schirach was promoted to the post of Reich Youth leader of the Nazi party, and the following year he grew closer to his beloved Führer when he married the 19-year-old Henriette Hoffman. The daughter of Hitler's personal photographer, she had grown up in a house to which he was a frequent visitor, and remembered one occasion well.

'After dinner Hitler – at that time he was still Herr Hitler to us – sat down at the piano and played some Wagner followed by some Verdi,' she recalled. 'He addressed me as Du [the informal form of 'you' in German], for I was only 17 and he was over 40. Then he took his leave and my father went with him.'

Henriette had worked as Hitler's

personal secretary before her marriage to Schirach, and the Führer had even dated her briefly. The marriage gained his warm approval, although it was opposed by Schirach's family.

Schirach had been marked out for advancement within the party, and in 1933, aged just 26, he was made head of the Hitler Youth, with Hitler calling on him to 'project National Socialism through German youth into eternity'.

The Hitler Youth, which had its roots in Hitler's Boy Storm Troop, an arm of the SA, had been founded in 1926. Originally purely a boys' movement, it had absorbed girls' groups and by 1933 Schirach was intent on bringing various other Nazi youth organisations under its wing.

At the end of 1932, shortly before Hitler came to power and Schirach was appointed to lead the organisation, it had 107,000 members. Schirach embarked on a massive recruitment drive and a year later membership had risen to 2.3 million. By 1940 the Hitler Youth had eight million members, with membership almost impossible to avoid for boys.

Children from the age of 10 could join the organisation, and they found themselves organised, in military fashion, into squads, platoons and companies. The emphasis for the boys was firmly on military training, with the aim of preparing them to fight for the Reich. Girls were prepared for the motherhood that would enable them to raise members for the party.

Both boys and girls were told they formed the start of the future Aryan super race, and part of their indoctrination involved the instilling of a viru-

To the Führer.

This is the truth which bound me to thee:
I looked for thee and found my Fatherland.
I was a leaf floating in limitless space.
Now thou art my homeland and my tree.
How far would I be carried by the wind,
Wert thou not the strength that flows
up from the roots.
I believe in thee, for thou art the nation.
I believe in Germany.
For thou art Germany's son.

BELOW The Hitler
Youth

lent anti-Semitism. Following Hitler's anti-intellectual stance, the boys' training majored on military and physical training at the expense of academic study.

Typical training activities included

BELOW The Hitler Youth

the weakest who would be of little use to the cause.

In the pre-war years the Nazis portrayed Schirach as an almost godlike figure and his image was to be seen everywhere – it nearly matched that of the Führer in its prominence. He worked tirelessly and with huge enthusiasm at his task of drilling into his young charges the concepts of discipline, character, obedience and leadership, as set out in his book Hitler Youth, published in 1934.

He continued to write his poems, too, and all of his work was infused with the message that the blood of Germany's youth was superior to that of all others.

an assault course and sessions in weapons training and tactical awareness. Bullying of younger and less able members was rife; it helped to identify

'Faust, the Ninth Symphony [of Beethoven] and the will of Adolf Hitler are eternal youth and know neither time nor transience,' was another

message. 'The body expresses our very being. The striving for beauty is inborn among the Aryan,' was another, aimed at the girls.

Despite his disdain for Judaism and an oft-expressed antipathy towards Christianity and its churches, Schirach exhorted Hitler Youth members to strive to serve God. 'He who serves our Führer, Adolf Hitler, serves Germany, and he who serves Germany, serves God,' he said.

But towards the end of the 1930s his exalted position at the head of a huge and vitally important organisation, and as one of Hitler's favourites, was being undermined. Martin Bormann was up to his usual intrigues, and scurrilous stories circulated of Schirach's effeminacy and his white bedroom decorated in a manner that did not tie in with the robustly masculine Nazi ideal he was promoting. In 1940, having organised the evacuation of five million children from areas that were vulnerable to Allied bombing raids, he joined the army.

His service at the front was distinguished if short-lived. Schirach's valour in France was rewarded with the Iron Cross Second Class but he was soon recalled to Germany. Losing his position as the leader of the Hitler Youth to Artur Axmann, he was posted to Austria as governor and gauleiter (regional Nazi party leader) of Vienna.

Here again, his star proved to be on the wane. He remained in Vienna until the end of the war and was responsible for the deportation of 65,000 Jews to Poland during that time, describing it as 'a contribution to European culture'.

But Bormann was up to his old tricks, manoeuvring against the younger man in private. Moreover, Schirach did not help his cause in Hitler's eyes when he travelled to the Berghof, the Führer's house in the Obersalzberg of the Bavarian Alps, to plead for the Jews to be transported in better conditions and for more humane treatment of the peoples of eastern Europe.

In pleading his case, Schirach found an ally in his wife. In 1943 Henriette witnessed the rounding-up of Jewish women in Amsterdam, and was shocked. She recalled: 'I was told that Jewish women were being deported, and didn't I know about it? My friends advised me to take the matter up with Hitler himself.'

This she did. At the Berghof she told

her old friend of the distressing scenes she had seen and asked if he knew about the deportations. 'A painful stillness fell; all colour had left Hitler's face,' she remembered. 'His face looked like a death mask in the light of the flames. He looked at me aghast and at the same time surprised and said: "We are at war."'

'At that moment he screamed at me: "You are sentimental, Frau von Schirach! You have to learn to hate! What have Jewish women in Holland got to do with you?"

'I walked out of the room and once in the vestibule began to run. One of Hitler's adjutants came running after me. The Führer was furious. I was asked to leave the Obersalzberg immediately.'

Neither Henriette nor her husband ever went back to the Berghof. Schirach had fallen into disfavour and there was no way back. His rapid rise to the status of a quasi-deity and intimate of the Führer had been mirrored by a descent to relative obscurity.

Schirach surrendered to the Allies in 1945 and went on trial at Nuremberg, charged with crimes against humanity. During the proceedings he exhibited a remarkable change of heart with regard

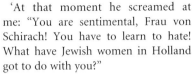

LEFT Transportation of Jews

to his feelings towards Jews, Nazism and Hitler.

He recognised that he had misled the youth of his country, contributing to the brainwashing of a generation, and admitted that he had ordered the deportation of Jews. 'I put my morals to one side when, out of misplaced faith in the Führer, I took part in this action,' he said. 'I did it. I cannot undo it.'

He denied that he knew anything at the time about the Nazis' death camps and described Auschwitz, whose horrors he had subsequently discovered, as 'the most devilish mass murder in history' and 'the most all-encompassing and diabolical genocide ever committed by man.

'Adolf Hitler gave the order. Hitler and Himmler together started this crime against humanity which will remain a blot on our history for centuries.' Hitler was a 'million-fold murderer', Schirach pronounced.

Despite his about-turn, the trial's prosecutors pushed hard for his conviction. The British prosecutor described his crimes: 'Schirach corrupted millions of German children so that they became what they really are today, the blind instruments of that policy of murder and domination which these men have carried out.'

And the American prosecutor Robert Jackson pressed the point. 'Von Schirach, poisoner of a generation, initiated the German youth in Nazi doctrine, trained them in legions for service in the SS and Wehrmacht and delivered them up to the party as fanatic, unquestioning executors of its will,' he said.

Schirach was sentenced to 20 years in Spandau Prison and, on his release in 1966, lived a quiet life in south-western Germany. He lived alone, for Henriette had divorced him while he was serving his sentence.

Around the time of the divorce, he was described thus in the New Central European Observer magazine: 'Baldur von Schirach was guilty of far more than war crimes. His was the deadly evil of corrupting the young. He poisoned the minds of an entire German generation. He trained and schooled the SS men, the men of the gas vans, the men of Auschwitz and Majdanek.'

Schirach lived in freedom for eight years, dying on 8 August 1974. He died almost totally blind – as blind as he had been to the truth in his earlier life.

Von Ribbentrop -
The Diplomat of Evil

Vain, arrogant, pompous, deluded, ignorant, duplicitous, ridiculous, power-mad, sycophantic, incompetent, a fool … neither historians nor his comrades in the Nazi party were especially kind when it came to describing Ulrich Friedrich Wilhelm Joachim von Ribbentrop.

He was the foreign minister who knew little of foreign affairs and nothing of foreign policy, according to the chief American prosecutor at Nuremberg, Robert H Jackson. He was a very superficial man in the view of Hitler's translator, Paul O Schmidt.

Ribbentrop's failings did not, however, prevent him from rising to the top in pre-war Germany, serving as Foreign Minister to the Nazi government and conducting negotiations with numerous foreign powers. Everywhere he went he did his damnedest to please his lord and master, Hitler.

Frequently – certainly as far as Germany's enemies were concerned – Ribbentrop's diplomatic missions failed. Yet somehow he clung on to his place at Hitler's side.

As the inevitable war dragged on, Ribbentrop's role and influence diminished; after all, what was a foreign minister expected to do when most of the world was engaged in fighting his country? But the Nuremberg judges still found him guilty of heinous crimes, and he became the first Nazi politician to be hanged.

"*The Jews in Germany were without exception pickpockets, murderers and thieves.*"

Joachim Ribbentrop, the son of a career officer who was later expelled from the army, was born on 30 April 1893 in Wesel, a city in the Rhenish province of Prussia. Assessed by one of his teachers as 'the most stupid in his class, full of vanity and very pushy', as a young man he nevertheless managed to pick up enough French and English to get by in those countries, as well as in Switzerland.

But it was in Canada that he found employment, working as a timekeeper on the rebuilding of the Quebec Bridge and the Canadian Pacific Railroad. He followed this with a spell as a journalist in New York and Boston before returning to Canada and setting up a business importing German wine.

ABOVE Collapse of the centre span of the Quebec Bridge

Thinking his presence in Canada unwise when World War I broke out in 1914, Ribbentrop returned to Germany and enlisted in the 125th Hussar Regiment. Serving first on the eastern front and then in the west, he earned a commission to officer rank and was decorated with the Iron Cross. He suffered a serious injury in 1917 before seeing out the war in Turkey at the rank of First Lieutenant. He was a member of the German delegation that attended the Paris Peace Conference at the end of the war.

Ribbentrop's post-war career began in the wine industry, thanks to his marriage to the daughter of a wealthy spar-kling wine producer. His work as he travelled around Europe was perhaps eased by the fact that he had added the aristocratic 'von' to his name, after persuading his aunt Gertrud von Ribbentrop to adopt him. In his role as wine salesman he was introduced in 1928 to Adolf Hitler as a businessman who got the same price for German sparkling wine as others got for French champagne.

It was a meeting that was to have highly important consequences for Germany's relations with foreign pow-ers throughout the 1930s, but it was not repeated until 1932, when Ribbentrop joined the Nazi party. The effect of that second meeting with Hitler was, Ribbentrop said later, instant and stunning.

'I was truly under Hitler's spell, that cannot be denied,' he told the psychiatrist Leon Goldensohn in 1946. 'I was impressed with him from the moment I first met him in 1932. He had terrific power, especially in his eyes.

'Hitler always, until the end, and even now, had a strange fascination over me. Would you call it abnormal of me? Sometimes, in his presence, when he spoke of all his plans, the good things he would do for the Volk, vacations, highways, new buildings, cultural advantages and so forth, tears would come to my eyes. Would that

BELOW Von Ribbentrop with Croatian fascist leader Ante Pavelic

be because I'm a hysterical weak man?'

Such was Hitler's effect on Ribbentrop that he was said to suffer psychosomatic illnesses if the Führer expressed his dissatisfaction with him. But in 1933 the Führer was far from unhappy, bestowing on Ribbentrop the honorary SS officer rank of Standartenführer and the role of foreign affairs adviser. This was despite the fact that Ribbentrop knew precious little, if anything at all, about the subject.

He had inveigled his way into the inner circle of Nazis who gathered round Hitler and sought his favours, and he had made enemies on the way. He was loathed by nearly all of his contemporaries, and Joseph Goebbels dismissed his reputation with the words: 'Ribbentrop bought his name, he married his money and he swindled his way into office.'

Ribbentrop fought back against his enemies, and improved his relationship with Hitler, by adopting a savagely anti-Semitic stance. This astonished many old colleagues to whom he previously had appeared a moderate.

There was nothing moderate about the views he expressed now, though. The writer Michael Bloch quoted him as saying to French Foreign Minister Georges Bonnet, when asked why Jews could not take their possessions with them when they left Germany: 'The Jews in Germany were without exception pickpockets, murderers and thieves. The property they possessed had been acquired illegally.'

At first denied the role he coveted – that of Foreign Minister – Ribbentrop took the extraordinary step of carrying out his own diplomatic missions and, in 1934, establishing the Ribbentrop Bureau, a kind of parallel ministry. He was rewarded for his initiative when Hitler appointed him to the prestigious role of ambassador to London in 1936.

Duped by Ribbentrop's endless flattery into thinking he had an exceptionally able diplomat who would bring

FAR LEFT Joachim von Ribbentrop as German ambassador to the United Kingdom

LEFT Soviet Foreign Minister Molotov signs the German-Soviet non-aggression pact; Joachim von Ribbentrop and Josef Stalin stand behind him, Moscow, 23 August 1939

home the prize he coveted most – an alliance with Britain against the threat of the Soviet Union – Hitler had unwittingly placed him in precisely the position where he could do most damage to Germany.

Extraordinary stories of Ribbentrop's time in London are legion. There is the one about him nearly knocking King George VI flying with a Nazi salute as the monarch stepped forward to shake his hand. There is the one about him posting SS guards outside the German Embassy and flying swastika flags on official cars.

There are stories about him keeping London's finest tailors waiting all day to take his measurements, only to be told Ribbentrop was too busy and to come back the following day. The disgruntled tailors passed on their grievances to their aristocratic clients, ensuring the latter would take a dislike to the arrogant ambassador. That was unfortunate for Ribbentrop, who courted the aristocracy assiduously in the mistaken belief that they – as well as the king – were influential in the formation of foreign policy.

His chaotic working practices were recalled by a member of his staff, who told Bloch: 'He rose, muttering bad-temperedly. Dressed in his pyjamas, he received the junior secretaries and press attachés in his bathroom.

'He scolded, threatened, gesticulated with his razor and shouted at his valet. As he took his bath he ordered people to be summoned from Berlin, accepted and cancelled, appointed and dismissed, and dictated through the door to a nervous stenographer …

'It was my task to put his calls

through; his valet stood within splashing distance holding a white telephone … Ribbentrop believed only ministers ranked above him; everyone else, including his ambassadorial colleagues, had to be kept waiting on the line. Sometimes they did not share this view and rang off.'

Ribbentrop became a figure of ridicule in London. His pompous behaviour in the corridors of power and his frequent visits to Germany prompted Punch magazine to dub him the Wandering Aryan. Nevertheless, his time in Britain did not go entirely to waste.

Although his blustering, forceful manner made it plain that he was entirely lacking in diplomatic skills, he achieved some success with the signing of the Anglo-German Naval Agreement in 1935. This was meant to regulate the size of the German navy in relation to its British counterpart.

After that, there was nothing. Ribbentrop's efforts to persuade Britain to sign an alliance with Germany against the Communist threat came to naught. He and Hitler had failed to understand that Britain had no interest in an alliance; at that point it was, instead, intent on the policy of appeasing Germany in the hope that it would not go to war.

Ribbentrop returned to Berlin a bitter, disillusioned man, albeit one who had been undone partly by his own incompetence. He was placated somewhat in February 1938 when Germany's Foreign Minister, Constantin von Neurath, was sacked and he was appointed to succeed him. Hitler saw him as more willing than Neurath to carry out his new foreign policy; a policy that would lead to war. And anything that Hitler demanded, Ribbentrop was delighted to do.

It was on Ribbentrop's watch that the Munich Agreement, agreeing to the German annexation of the Sudetenland areas of Czechoslovakia, was signed in September 1938. He played a key role in the signing of the Treaty of Non-Aggression between Germany and the Soviet Union, also known as the Molotov-Ribbentrop Pact. 'I rather liked Stalin and Molotov (the Soviet Foreign Minister), got along fine with them,' he recalled in 1946.

The Soviet-German pact meant little to Hitler, however, and in 1940, considering the invasion of the Soviet Union, he sent Ribbentrop to negotiate a treaty

VON RIBBENTROP

BELOW Detention report and mugshots of Joachim Von Ribbentrop

with Japan. On 25 September the Nazi Foreign Minister sent a telegram to Molotov informing him that Germany was about to form a military alliance, with Japan and Italy, that would direct its efforts against the United States, not the Soviet Union.

In fact Molotov already knew about the pact, but he did not know much detail about Hitler's Operation Barbarossa – the Nazi invasion of the Soviet Union – until December 1940. The invasion was launched on 22 June 1941. Duplicitous to a fault, Hitler and

Ribbentrop had attempted to deceive the Soviets while condemning to death up to 30 million troops and civilians on both sides.

Thereafter, Ribbentrop faded into the background; there was not much diplomacy to be done anyway, as Germany had diplomatic relations with just a handful of countries, some of them puppet states. In addition, Hitler had tired of Ribbentrop, who spent his time battling with other Nazis over control of the party's anti-Semitic policies.

In April 1945 Ribbentrop attended

BELOW Detention report and mugshots of Joachim Von Ribbentrop

DETENTION REPORT

File number

SEX (1)

(M F

Ring applicable

Office use only

Surname : RIBBENTROP

First names : Joachim von

Aliases : Riese, Johann

Civil Occupation : German Government

Nationality : German (2)

VON RIBBENTROP JOACHIM 31G 350052 23 JUNE 1945

Do not write in shaded portions

DATE OF BIRTH (3)	PLACE OF BIRTH (3a)	WEIGHT (3b)	HEIGHT (4)
April 1893	Wesel/Rhine	82 Kgs	1.78m

the Führer's 56th birthday celebrations. The next time he tried to make arrangements to see Hitler, he was told brusquely to go away.

He was arrested the following month near Hamburg. In his possession was a letter addressed to 'Vincent' Churchill, blaming the misnamed Prime Minister for the advance of Bolshevism into central Europe. Ribbentrop, it appeared, was so ignorant of foreign affairs that he did not know the name of the British wartime leader.

At Nuremberg, Ribbentrop was accused of crimes against peace and against humanity, waging a war of aggression and war crimes. The American prosecutor Robert H Jackson told the judges: 'When apprehensions abroad threatened the success of the Nazi regime for conquest, it was the duplicitous Ribbentrop, the salesman of deception, who was detailed to pour wine on the troubled waters of suspicion by preaching the gospel of limited and peaceful intentions.'

For his part, Ribbentrop attempted to blame Hitler alone for the fate of the Jews. 'I know for a fact that this idea of the Jews causing the war and the Jews being so all-important is nonsense,' he told Leon Goldensohn. 'But that was Hitler's idea, and was pure fantasy ... Hitler is a riddle to me and will always remain so.' Strange words for a man who had admitted that he had wept while listening to the Führer expound his plans.

Ribbentrop was found guilty of all charges and sentenced to death. He was hanged on 16 October 1946.

Bizarrely for someone who had paved the way to worldwide conflict, his last words were reported to be: 'My last wish is that Germany realise its entity and that an understanding be reached between East and West. I wish peace to the world.'

BELOW Ribbentrop's body after execution

Chapter 11

Mengele -
The Doctor of Death

There are few words in the English language sufficiently adequate to describe the inhuman cruelty inflicted by Dr Josef Mengele on his victims in the Auschwitz death camp.

From May 1943 until the end of the war, Mengele drugged, castrated, stitched together, injected, infected, froze, performed surgery without anaesthetics, transfused, amputated, killed and dissected. His human guinea pigs all served as subjects in his quest to further genetic knowledge and help to create an Aryan super race.

Mengele is known by several nicknames – the Doctor of Death, the White Angel, the Angel of Death – but none is sufficient to convey the horror of the crimes he committed. A Jew-hater and a committed Nazi, he seemed to take delight in selecting victims for his macabre experiments, especially if they happened to be twins.

He even managed to escape the justice that was meted out at Nuremberg to so many of his Nazi comrades. At the war's end he went on the run, ending up in South America. And there he stayed, living under a succession of false names, until he died a rather ordinary death in 1979. How his victims would have welcomed an ordinary death.

Born on 16 March 1911 in the Bavarian city of Günzburg, to an industrialist father whose company continues to sell farm machinery to this day, Mengele grew to be a cultured, good-

"*The more we do to you, the less you seem to believe we are doing it.*"

looking figure who was popular in the town. When he left for the University of Munich, it was to study physical anthropology, but he later switched to the Institute for Hereditary Biology and Racial Hygiene in Frankfurt. Here he worked under Otmar von Verschuer, a scientist who was renowned for his work in genetics with a particular interest in twins. It was an interest that Mengele shared.

His PhD in anthropology, gained in 1935, gave further clues as to his future career path – it was entitled A Racial-Morphological Examination of the Anterior Portion of the Lower Jaw in Four Racial Groups. Mengele followed this up with further publications, on the genealogical study of cases of cleft

DR JOSEF MENGELE

BELOW Mengele
(left) in SS uniform

lip, jaw and palate; the hereditary transmission of defects in the human ear; and the 'irregular, dominant hereditary process'.

Mengele's interest in heredity and genetics tied in conveniently with the ideology of his chosen political party, the Nazis. He was apparently intent on helping in the creation of the racially 'pure', blue-eyed Aryan super-race the Nazi leaders expected and demanded.

He joined the party in 1937 and immediately applied for membership of the SS. His academic work was interrupted in 1938/9 by military matters: he served six months with a light infantry regiment specialising in mountain warfare, later volunteering for service in the medical department of the Waffen-SS, the fighting arm of the organisation.

Mengele showed immense bravery

BELOW Mengele (left) in SS uniform

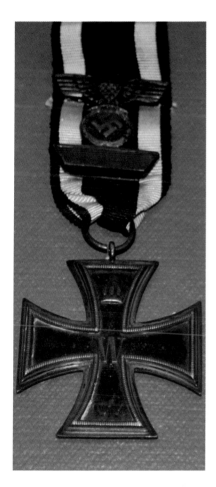

in combat. In 1941 he was awarded the Iron Cross Second Class for his heroism on the Ukrainian front, and the following year, after fighting behind the Soviet lines, he earned the Iron Cross First Class and the Medal for the Care of the German People. This was awarded for his bravery in pulling two comrades from a burning tank.

His military career was at an end, however. He had received an injury that was serious enough for him to be declared medically unfit for combat, and he was posted to the Race and Resettlement Office – responsible for safeguarding the racial 'purity' of the SS – in Berlin. He was later quoted as saying: 'There can't be two smart peoples in the world. We're going to win the war, so only the Aryan race will stand.'

Mengele also took up his former studies again, working under Von Verschuer at the Kaiser Wilhelm Institute for Anthropology, Human Genetics and Eugenics.

By this time he had received further recognition of his outstanding service to the SS by being promoted to the rank of Captain. That award came shortly before a doctor at the Auschwitz death camp in Poland fell ill and his posi-

DR JOSEF MENGELE

RIGHT A Death's
Head SS cap

tion became vacant. Mengele saw an unparalleled opportunity for furthering his studies through live experimentation on human beings. He moved to Auschwitz in May 1943.

It is often stated that Mengele was the chief medical officer at Auschwitz. In fact that dubious honour belonged to another, but Mengele certainly acted as if he owned the place.

Immaculately groomed, with a riding crop in his right hand, his boots highly polished and his Death's Head SS cap set at a rakish angle, he strode about the camp on his deadly business. One inmate recalled: 'He had a look that said: "I am the power".'

Mengele's favourite task was the selection, from the prisoners who arrived regularly at the camp railway station, of those who would die immediately and those who would live a while longer.

The few people who survived Auschwitz remembered his awe-inspiring resemblance to his 'White Angel' nickname as he stood, white-coated with arms outstretched, on the platform, indicating which direction the new arrivals should take. Left led the condemned straight to the gas chambers; right took prisoners to a

short, brutal life of starvation, living conditions of extreme harshness and unceasing, backbreaking labour.

Nothing excited Mengele more than the discovery on the platform of a pair of twins. He would push through the crowds, former inmates recalled, shouting 'Zwillinge heraus! Zwillinge heraustreten! (Twins out! Twins step forward!).'

Twins were marked out for special treatment in accommodation that was slightly better than the norm at Auschwitz, with larger food rations and always the possibility of sugar or a sweet or two from the smiling Uncle Mengele. The favoured inmates chosen by Mengele during his 21-month stay numbered 3,000 twins – 1,500 pairs, in other words. Some were as young as five.

Other people he chose to separate from the gas chamber victims did not live such privileged lives as the twins, if they lived at all. Those who suffered from bodily deformities or other anomalies – hunchbacks, dwarfs and giants among them – were usually killed as soon as they arrived and dissected for Mengele's study. Perhaps they were lucky to die. They would

surely not have preferred the living hell through which the Doctor of Death put other experimental subjects.

He injected chemicals into children's eyes to see if they would change colour. He castrated twins, he sterilised them, he performed sex change operations on them. He injected them with deadly bacteria, he amputated limbs and removed organs, often without anaesthesia. He transfused blood from one twin to another, he stitched children's blood vessels and organs together in an attempt to create conjoined twins. He froze children to death, he put them in pressure chambers, he performed electroconvulsive therapy on them.

And when he was sure that his victims were no longer of any use to him alive – if they had not died already – Mengele killed them, dissected them and studied the effects of what he had done.

One night, a survivor remembered, one of Mengele's assistants rounded up 14 pairs of twins, all Romani people from eastern Europe. 'Mengele placed them on his polished marble dissection table and put them to sleep,' she continued. 'He then injected chloroform into their hearts, killing them instantly. Mengele then began dissecting and meticulously noting each piece of the twins' bodies.'

The assistant the survivor mentioned was no Nazi; neither was he working willingly. Mengele's helpers were chosen from among the Auschwitz population for their skills or knowledge and given the precious chance to live in return for helping Mengele in his inhuman work. He gave them the choice: help me or die.

When Auschwitz was liberated by Red Army troops on 27 January 1945, they were greeted by the sight of hundreds of children inside the perimeter wire of the camp. These were the survivors of Mengele's experiments.

Among them were identical twins Eva Mozes Kor and Miriam Mozes, who had been deported from a small village in Romania. Eva later recalled that when they arrived at Auschwitz with their mother, a guard noticed that she and her sister looked alike. 'Are they twins?' he asked their mother. 'Is that good?' she replied. The guard nodded. 'They are twins,' she confirmed.

Miriam and Eva were snatched from their mother. 'Our screams fell on deaf ears,' said Eva. 'I remember looking back and seeing my mother's arms stretched out in despair as we were led away by a soldier. That was the last time I saw her.'

The brutal realities of life at Auschwitz did not take long to come to light. The first time Eva went to the latrine she was confronted by the sight of several children's corpses scattered on the floor. She vowed there and then that she and her sister would not end their lives the same way.

Then came Mengele's experiments, one of which Eva recalled vividly. 'I was given five injections,' she said. 'That evening I developed extremely high fever. I was trembling. My arms and legs were swollen, huge size.

'Mengele and Dr Konig and three other doctors came in the next morning. They looked at my fever chart and Dr Mengele said, laughingly: "Too bad, she is so young. She has only two weeks to live."'

Eva remembered a pair of Roma twins who were sewn back to back: Mengele's attempt to create conjoined twins by connecting blood vessels and organs. In agony and terror, the twins screamed incessantly for three days and nights until they were freed from their ordeal by the onset of gangrene and the

DR JOSEF MENGELE

BELOW Child survivors of Auschwitz, 1945

resulting death.

Mengele carried out countless experiments and procedures on living and dead human beings. We have seen that he was fascinated by genetics and heredity, and that he was committed, as a faithful Nazi, to the creation of the 'Aryan' super race. But was he as serious in his work as he seemed?

One Auschwitz inmate who lived to tell his tale, Alex Dekel, was convinced he was not. 'I have never accepted the fact that Mengele himself believed he was doing serious work – not from the slipshod way he went about it,' he said. 'He was only exercising his power.

'Mengele ran a butcher shop – major surgeries were performed without anaesthesia. Once I witnessed a stomach operation. Mengele was removing pieces from the stomach but without any anaesthetic. Another time it was a heart that was removed, again without anaesthesia. It was horrifying.'

Dekel continued: 'Mengele was a doctor who became mad because of the power he was given. Nobody ever questioned him – why did this one die? Why did that one perish? The patients did not count.

'He professed to do what he did in the name of science, but it was a madness on his part.'

We cannot know for sure if Dekel was right. Most historians have accepted that there was method in Mengele's madness and he was trying to bring to light the knowledge that would benefit his Nazi masters. But no investigator ever got an answer from the Angel of

Death, because he disappeared.

How he managed to vanish is a mystery, because he was in the custody of American forces, under his own name, at one time in 1945. He was released, however, in June of that year with papers giving his name as Fritz Hollman. From then until 1949 he is thought to have lived and worked as a farm labourer in a Bavarian village.

Then it is thought he escaped, with the help of his wife Irene and friend Hans Sedlmeier, to Argentina. There he got to know other Nazis on the run from justice and resumed his medical career, specialising, it is said, in illegal abortions. Moving on to Paraguay and then Brazil, using further false names, Mengele always managed to stay one step ahead of Mossad and other intelligence agencies.

Mengele died on 7 February 1979 when he apparently suffered a stroke while swimming in the Atlantic Ocean off São Paulo. At the time he was known as Wolfgang Gerhard.

His death came 19 years after Sedlmeier had returned from Paraguay with a statement from the fugitive Mengele. In response to accusations of the hideous crimes he had committed, he said: 'I personally have not killed, injured or caused bodily harm to anyone.'

The Hippocratic Oath, sworn by doctors throughout the world, states: 'I will apply dietetic measures for the benefit of the sick according to my ability and judgment; I will keep them from harm and injustice.'

Perhaps Dr Mengele omitted to swear that part of the oath.

BELOW Josefe Mengele's former home in Hohenau, Itapua, Paraguay. Photo taken August 2007

Chapter 12

Freisler -

The Arbitrator over Death & Life

In most legal systems, judges are supposed to be impartial, independent arbiters who will weigh the evidence carefully before ensuring justice is done, freeing the innocent and sanctioning the guilty. That was not Roland Freisler's way.

The President of the Nazis' so-called People's Court had his own justice system, one in which the word 'justice' was a misnomer. Freisler acted as prosecutor, judge and jury as he dealt with opponents of the totalitarian regime he represented.

Ranting, bawling, howling, screaming, shouting down the pleas of the accused and their lawyers – if they had any lawyers worthy of the name – he savagely denounced their monstrous 'crimes'. He humiliated and abused them, then, more often that not, he pronounced that they had forfeited their lives and sent them to their deaths.

The number of death sentences imposed by the People's Court rocketed when Freisler was in charge. He handed down his judgments with instructions like 'off with his head', as if emulating the Queen of Hearts in his own private Wonderland. Then he justified his own decisions in the court records with convoluted logic worthy of any other Lewis Carroll character.

Freisler's end came during an Allied bombing raid on Berlin. Justice had come from the heavens.

There is some debate over the exact

HITLER'S HENCHMEN

"*If you have nothing to say for yourself then kindly keep your mouth shut.*"

circumstances of Roland Freisler's death and, rather fittingly, not much is known about his early life either. We do know, however, that he was born the son of an engineer in Celle, Lower Saxony in north-western Germany, on 30 October 1893. He served his country in World War I, rising from the status of an officer cadet in 1914 to the rank of Lieutenant in 1915, and earning the Iron Cross, both First and Second Class, along the way.

His war ended soon after when, having been wounded in battle in October 1915, he was captured by the imperial Russian army. Freisler spent the rest of the conflict as a prisoner of war and made the most of his time by learning Russian. He is also thought to

ROLAND FREISLER

have developed an interest in Marxism following the events of 1917, when the Tsarist autocracy was blown away in the Russian Revolution. Some sources state that Freisler became a communist.

Bolshevik revolutionaries had certainly used him as a 'commissar' for his PoW camp's food supplies, but the historian HW Koch has stated that the title was simply functional and had no political overtones. After the war the camps were administered by German authorities, he added, and although when he joined the Nazi party Freisler tended towards its left wing, he was never a communist.

Despite denying that he ever collaborated with Bolsheviks, however, Freisler was never able to rid himself of the 'bolshie' label.

By 1920 Freisler was back in Germany, studying law at the University of Jena and earning the title of Doctor of Law in 1922. From 1924 he practised law in Kassel, in the Hesse region of central Germany, and was elected as a city councillor representing the nationalist People's Social Block.

Despite what were perceived as his leftish tendencies, he joined the Nazi party in July 1925 and set about defending members of the party who had fallen foul of the law of the Weimar Republic. Those who saw him defending his clients in court could not fail to be impressed by Freisler's powers of oratory, nimble thinking and mastery of the law.

By this time a member of the Prussian state legislature – he was later also elected to the Reichstag – Freisler was marked out for future use by a Nazi party that was readying itself for a surge towards power. One Gauleiter (regional leader) noted in 1927: 'Rhetorically Freisler is equal to our best speakers, if not superior. Particularly on the broad masses, he has influence, but thinking people mostly reject him.

'Party Comrade Freisler is only usable as a speaker. He is unsuitable for any leadership post, since he is an unreliable and moody person.'

Freisler was regarded as a lone operator, and he had no influential patron to speak up for him and advance his position in the party. His career was also limited by the actions of his lawyer brother Oswald, who annoyed Nazis by wearing his party badge while defending clients in trials of political significance. Since the party wanted to focus on these trials for propaganda purposes, such a blatant show of loyalty confused the Nazi message, and propaganda chief Joseph Goebbels is believed to have given Roland Freisler a dressing-down over his brother's actions. Oswald was also expelled from the party.

In addition, Freisler was not liked by his party comrades. (One often wonders if any of the scheming, self-serving Nazi leaders had anyone they could call a friend among their peers.) Goebbels was certainly appreciative of Freisler's skills, but he was brusquely rebuffed when he proposed that he should be the successor to Justice Minister Franz Gürtner. 'That old Bolshevik? No!' said Hitler.

In spite of Hitler's dismissal of him, Freisler's loyalty to the Nazi cause could not be questioned, and he was a much-feared judge who contributed to the regime's oppressive nature.

Even if he would never reach the upper echelons of the Nazi hierarchy, his ascent began in February 1933 – just weeks before Hitler gained his dictatorial powers – when he was appointed department head in the Prussian Ministry of Justice. In 1933 and 1934

he served as State Secretary in that Ministry, and from 1934 to 1942 with the same title in the Reich Ministry of Justice.

And Freisler made a large contribution to the Nazi state's lawmaking process. In 1939 he published an article called The Racial-Biological Task Involved in the Reform of Juvenile Criminal Law, calling for 'racially foreign, racially degenerate, racially incur-able or seriously defective juveniles' to be sent to educational centres where their wayward beliefs could be corrected. They should be separated from those who were 'racially valuable', he argued.

The same year he paved the way for the death penalty to be imposed on juveniles for the first time in Germany's history with his Juvenile Felons Decree. In September of that year Freisler sup-

LEFT The Volksgerichtshof: Reinecke, Freisler, Lautz

BELOW Roland Freisler and Heinrich Lautz

RIGHT Just one of the death sentences handed out by Freisler

ported the Decree against National Parasites, which deemed juvenile crime to be parasitic in nature. 'In times of war, breach of loyalty and baseness cannot find any leniency and must be met with the full force of the law,' he announced.

He was also a strong supporter of the state's laws prohibiting 'race defilement' – sexual relations between the 'Aryan' race and 'inferior' ones. He went further, outlining in a pamphlet his view that sex with any foreigner, regardless of his or her 'inferiority' or 'superiority', should be banned.

It was inevitable that Freisler would make an indelible mark on the legal system, and his chance came on 20 August 1942, when Hitler appointed him President of the People's Court.

The Volksgerichtshof had been established in Berlin in 1934, outside the normal boundaries of the law, as a means of dealing with the vast number of political offences the Nazis judged injurious to their interests. Political dissent existed in Nazi Germany; it simply never had much chance to flourish before it was crushed with lethal efficiency.

The court dealt with crimes like black marketeering and industrial action as if they were the political acts of parasites of the state. At the top of Freisler's hate list were incidences of 'defeatism', which was ruled to have a negative effect on the Nazis' defensive capability. In reality, just about any offence could be described as political.

A typical pronouncement from Freisler's bench went something like this: 'The accused called in handbills for the sabotage of armaments and for the fall of the National Socialist way of life of our people, publicised defeatist thoughts and insulted the Führer in a detestable way.'

Any defendant brought before the court knew he or she had little chance of being found not guilty – verdicts and sentences were often agreed beforehand – and every chance of being condemned to death, either on the gallows or at the guillotine. Even if you were a first-time or infrequent offender, or merely a petty criminal, the chances were your time was up.

Nine out of ten cases, even those involving juveniles, resulted in a sentence of death or life imprisonment, and under Freisler's jurisdiction the death penalty was evoked with extraordinary regularity.

Between 1942 and 1945, he handed down no fewer than 2,600 death sentences, out of a total in that period of 5,000. He was responsible in his three years for more than half of the death sentences pronounced in the entire life of the court.

And Freisler often chose to pass the death sentence in a bizarre way, shouting 'The beet must be uprooted!' or 'Off with his head!'

But he became just as notorious for the way he conducted proceedings as for his premeditated verdicts and sentences. Freisler rarely gave a defendant or his state-appointed lawyer the chance to defend himself, shouting down any attempt to justify or mitigate. He bullied, he abused and he humiliated.

At the trial of those involved in the July Bomb Plot to assassinate Hitler, the men were dressed in shabby clothes and denied ties and trouser belts, forcing them to stand awkwardly in the dock clutching their trousers for fear they would fall down and cause further humiliation. They were in court, Freisler declared, to face 'the most horrific charges ever brought in the history of the German people'.

Beglaubigte Abschrift.
================================

In der Strafsache gegen den vom Sondergericht in Bremen am 8. Juli 1942 als Volksschädling wegen Brandstiftung zum Tode verurteilten

Walerjan W r o b e l

habe ich mit Ermächtigung des Führers beschlossen, von dem Begnadigungsrecht keinen Gebrauch zu machen, sondern der Gerechtigkeit freien Lauf zu lassen.

Berlin, den   15. August 1942
Der Reichsminister der Justiz
In Vertretung
(Siegel)   gez. Dr. Freisler

Mit der Urschrift gleichlautend:
Berlin, den 17.August 1942

als Ministerialkanzleiobersekretär.

One defendant, dressed in a cardi-
gan, was addressed by Freisler as a
Schweinehund (pig-dog). When he
could get a word in and protest that he
was not such an animal, Freisler coolly
asked him in which zoological category
he would class himself.

It is worth noting here that the 50 tri-

als of those suspected of being involved in the July Bomb Plot – which were recorded for posterity on film – resulted in more than 110 death sentences.

After one of the trials over which he presided, having meted out his brutal concept of justice, Judge-Jury-Prosecutor Freisler would retire to complete his paperwork, recording his verdicts and sentences. These he filled with as much crass Nazi ideology as he could, justifying his actions on the grounds, more likely than not, that the defendant had been defeatist, thus undermining the German people's morale and aiding the enemy.

Freisler was quick to hand out judgments on other people; the judgment on his own life was too slow in coming to save the lives of thousands, but come it eventually did.

On Saturday, 3 February 1945, Freisler was going about his usual murderous business in the People's Court. All sources agree that Berlin came under attack from Allied bomber aircraft targeting government buildings at that time, but there are several versions of how Freisler was killed.

According to some he was crushed by a falling masonry column, still holding some files he had wanted to retrieve after adjourning and evacuating the court. Another version states he was killed when a bomb penetrated the courtroom ceiling as he was trying – and no doubt condemning – two women, who survived the blast.

A third version of events is that Freisler was fatally wounded by a bomb fragment while trying to escape from the courtroom and make his way to an air raid shelter. According to this account, he bled to death on the pavement outside the court building.

However he died, it is certain that his demise was mourned by no one apart from his family – certainly not by the petty criminals of Germany; the number of death sentences allocated at the People's Court fell dramatically.

Many years later, Louise Jodl, the wife of General Alfred Jodl, said she had been working at a Berlin hospital when Freisler's body was brought in. A hospital worker remarked: 'It is God's verdict.' And Mrs Jodl reported: 'Not one person said a word in reply.'

Freisler, the personification of Nazi Germany's blood justice, went to his unmarked grave unmourned.

LEFT Freisler with Justice Minister Franz Schlegelberger and jurists Otto Thierack and Curt Rothenberger

The pictures in this book were provided courtesy of the following:

WIKIMEDIA COMMONS
www.commons.wikimedia.org

Design & Artwork: ALEX YOUNG

Published by: DEMAND MEDIA LIMITED & G2 ENTERTAINMENT LIMITED

Publishers: JASON FENWICK & JULES GAMMOND

Written by: PATRICK MORGAN